Miss Adams, Country Teacher

Memories from a one-room school

Wind Springs School, 1928–29

Treva Adams Strait

Treva Adams,
age 18, in the
spring of 1928

All photos are from the collection of the author.

ISBN 0-934904-25-1

J & L Lee Co.
Postal Box 5575
Lincoln, NE 68505

Contents

Acknowledgments

This book would not have been published without the help of so many.

My husband, John Milton Strait, inspired me.

The writing class; Claire Accomando, Rose Marie Armentrout, Kathryn Avery, Dora Barr, Maria Budzynski, Fern Moore, Eila Perez, Bill Slinkard, Bill Talley, Mary Trimble, Nora West, encouraged and advised me.

Students during the years that this story covers reminded me of incidents and furnished materials. They were: Katherine Lind Miller, Alec Lind, Reuben Lind, Mary Snider Meyer, Harry Snider, Virginia Garlow Lewis, Donald and Douglas Beebe, Martha Propp Meisner, Esther Propp Schmidt, and Joan Hays McKerrigan.

Katherine Lind and David Miller gave consent for the account of their wedding.

My brother, Norman Adams, reminded me that Dad exchanged a cow for a Dodge car. After my brother's death, his widow, Opal, and three children Norman Jr., Roger and Suzanne gave permission to use his christian name, Norman. He was "Howard" in The Price Of Free Land.

My sisters Dorothy Adams Burden and Helen Adams Mauler added information.

Ray Burden researched materials concerning the closing of the banks in 1929.

Mrs. Roy Schaffer furnished a picture of Airport School and its history.

Patricia Strait Welch researched Bufton's Universal Cyclopaedia.

Glenn Woodworth explained the mechanics of the Model T.

Lorine Kaasch Baggs furnished pertinent information about the dance hall on her father's farm.

Daniel Ross, editor of University of Nebraska Press and Suzanne Jung, Chula Vista librarian, suggested additions.

I am indebted to Jerry Kromberg who read my manuscript and gave it to editor James McKee.

This book is dedicated
to
all who attended a one teacher rural school
and
especially those pupils I taught
from
1928 to 1952

WIND SPRINGS RANCH SCHOOL— MY FIRST SCHOOL

Nebraska, 1928

"I can't say 'ain't' any more," I said as I climbed through the barbed wire fence on my way to my first teaching job, on the western Nebraska prairie. Winter storms had left dirty snow drifted around fence posts and in ravines. The winds had exposed clumps of grey-green sagebrush and beaver tail cactus on the otherwise dreary landscape. A cold March wind slapped my face so hard tears stung my eyes. It blew my coat open and tugged at the pink and white gingham dress Mother had made last June for my eighteenth birthday.

My overshoes didn't seem heavy or clumsy as I ran and skipped along. I felt like flying. There was no doubt in my mind about being a good teacher. I'd planned for this day for years and now it was here.

Distances didn't bother me since I'd grown up on a ranch, but this was the longest three miles I'd ever walked. Was I going in the right direction? Finally as I climbed through the second fence a small building came into view. My school.

As I ran toward it, thoughts rushed back to the previous week when a middle-aged, small, wiry man drove into our yard. I looked out the kitchen window to watch him jump from his dilapidated Ford truck and stride toward the house.

Mother pushed a strand of hair aside before she opened the door. My hair was curly like hers, but dark brown instead of a pretty auburn. She could pass as my older sister with her slender figure and rosy cheeks. Dad said I resembled Mother with my brown eyes, though I didn't have her deep dimples. From Dad I'd inherited my hearty laugh, broad grin and the shape of my eyes.

"Good morning," Mother said to the stranger on the doorstep. "Can I help you?"

"I'm Ennis James, a rancher in Sioux County. I'm looking for Treva Adams. We need a teacher. There's six boys on my ranch who belong to my two cowboy helpers, so we got to have school."

I stepped beside Mother. My heart had flip-flopped when I heard my name and the words 'need a teacher.' I swallowed hard. "I'm Treva. Why are you looking for a teacher this time of year? It's nearly the first of March."

"Well, we ain't had no school yet." The man paused as though searching for the right words. "The fathers thought they was smart enough to learn their boys. County superintendent changed their minds. He was in our district last week, said we had to have a qualified teacher right away."

"How did you know about me?"

"Oh, I know your pa. He was tellin' me at a farm sale two weeks ago he had a smart, good-looking daughter who needed a teaching job. I'll pay you two hundred fifty dollars for three months' work."

I wanted to jump for joy. A job! "Mother, isn't that wonderful?"

She fingered her apron. "How far is it from here? Where will she stay during the week?"

Mr. James pushed his old felt hat back and held up his hand. "Whoa, one question at a time. She'll be about twenty-five miles from home. It's west past Gilbert's farm then north into the ranch country. There'll be nothing but prairie until she sees about a dozen trees near the road. She can't miss it. That's Wind Springs. That's where she'll stay."

Mother frowned. "Who will she live with?"

"No one."

I gasped. All my friends who taught in rural schools roomed and boarded with families in the community. My heart beat faster. I'd always bragged I never was afraid of anything, but this was different.

The man continued. "There's a cowboy's shack in the middle of them trees."

When I heard this, I blocked out the conversation. A shack. That probably meant a small, one-room frame building made of wood, covered with tar paper. It surely wouldn't be as warm and comfortable as our sod house.

Again I listened. "Ed Armstrong lives in the big house. He says he'll have his wife mop the floor, so it should be pretty clean. There's a bed, table, couple of chairs." He looked at me. "You'll have to bring a stove and what else you need."

"Are you sure it's safe for her to live alone?" I thought I detected a quiver in Mother's voice.

"Ma'am, the only thing that might bother her would be the howling of the coyotes at night. The Armstrong house is only a hundred yards away."

"Is the school there too?" I asked.

He shook his head. "Nope. It's three miles straight east. You'll go through a few valleys and over a couple of hills until you reach a fence. Then you'll see the schoolhouse." There was a glint in his eye as he asked, "Guess you know how to climb through a fence?"

I laughed. "I should. I've done it most of my life."

"The building is a shack cowboys used during branding time. A few years ago we needed it for a school. It's been a spell now since anybody used it." He paused. "Have I answered all your questions?"

I nodded. "I guess so. What do you think, Mother?"

She smiled and nodded.

"Then you'll take the job?"

Trying to keep my voice calm, I asked, "When do I begin?"

"Sooner the better. Next Monday?"

I gave Mother a quick glance to get her approval. "Yes, I'm sure I can be ready by then." I was so excited I wanted to shout the news to the world. Then I remembered Dad.

"Mr. James, don't leave. I'll be right back." I left on the run to find my handsome, blue-eyed father who was repairing harness in a small area of the barn that he called his shop. I grabbed him by the shoulders and yelled as though he were deaf, "Dad, come quick! I've got a job!"

He laid down a piece of leather.

"Come before he leaves." I clutched his sleeve and pulled him toward the door.

"Who's he? What kind of job?"

"Teaching, of course. Mr. James came to ask me. You won't have to spend any more money on me. I can pay my own way from now on."

He stopped, swung his hat in the air and yelled, "Whoopee! That's a relief. It's about time you were making your own way."

Mother and the visitor were talking in the front yard when we returned. The men shook hands.

"Well, Adams, when you spoke about your daughter, bet you didn't know there'd be action this quick."

"That's for sure. She's anxious to support herself. You got yourself a good teacher." A big smile showed my father's pride. "She's been playing school with her two younger sisters since she was knee-high to a grasshopper."

Mr. James glanced over at me. "I'm glad I got her." To me he added, "There's a supply of chalk and erasers, a broom and dustpan, and a load of coal that should last for three months." He stopped and cleared his throat. "Don't start the fire until it's real cold. The boys can wear their coats. The windows are on the east, west, and south, so when it's a clear day you should get enough heat from the sun." He paused. "Guess that's all. The boys'll expect you on Monday." As he turned and strode back to his truck he called over his shoulder, "Good-bye."

I watched him leave and gave myself a hug. Teaching was the only thing

3

I'd ever wanted to do. Maybe I could inspire those boys to achieve beyond their expectations or those of their parents. Mother had always said if we did our best in our schoolwork our classmates wouldn't look down on us because we were poor. Norman and I had both been members of the National Honorary Society and my two sisters were doing very well in school also.

Each year as we children grew up, Mother spent one full day visiting school. She and Dad had both talked to our teachers at the community meetings. I hoped the parents of these six boys would be as interested in them as my parents had been in us.

A job, money, fulfilling my hearts desire; life couldn't be better. If I had any concern it would be the thought of living alone.

Mother and Dad went into the house and settled into their favorite rockers. I followed and sat in a straightback chair opposite them.

"Dad, can you find a stove to heat a one-room shack? It has to have a flat top, so I can use it for cooking too."

He continued to rock. "We'll have to move pretty fast. I'll try to find one tomorrow at a secondhand store. Guess you and your mother can take care of everything else."

My forty-year-old mother arose, walked to a cupboard, picked up a pencil and paper and began to write. "It sure would help if we could see that room, but since that's impossible I'll jot down a few things I know you'll need."

"Mother, while you do that, I'll write to Norman. Won't he be pleased to learn that his sister finally has a job? He can brag about me to his fraternity brothers. And wait until Helen and Dorothy get home from school. Will they ever be surprised."

During the rest of the week, Mother helped me select my clothes, dishes, cooking utensils and other things I would need.

Sunday morning we packed my five-day supply of food. There was a loaf of homemade bread, a half pound of butter we had churned, cottage cheese, a pint of canned string beans, a few carrots from the cellar, a half dozen eggs, a few potatoes and slices of home-cured ham. Mother laid five apples and some oatmeal cookies on top of one box.

Just before we left, I took a gallon of milk from the ice box. Thanks to our cold winters, there was always plenty of ice from Lake Alice a half mile away to keep us well stocked. Dad dug a pit near the house to fill with ice every January or February. He covered it with straw to keep it from melting.

By one o'clock everything was loaded on our truck. "Don't forget to lock the door before you go to bed," Mother cautioned as she kissed me good-bye. My sisters hugged me. Dad shifted impatiently and looked relieved when we were on our way, at last.

The gravel road turned into a dusty trail after we reached the ranch country. It took an hour before we saw the big trees that Mr. James had mentioned.

The Armstrong's large unpainted ranch house with a porch across the entire front stood near the grove. It had no curtains or shades at the two big windows. We saw no one. It gave me an eerie feeling, as though I had come to a deserted place. The only other building was near the spring in the middle of the grove of trees, so this had to be my home. I hurried from the truck to inspect it. To my delight, I found the floor clean and still damp from being mopped. The table and two straight chairs needed paint, but had been dusted.

When Dad entered he said, "This building isn't covered with tar paper, only board and batting." Then he patted the wall with his open palm. "This is the outside board. You'll probably be wishing for three-foot thick walls like our soddy." He rubbed his hands together. "It sure is cold in here."

I nodded. "Mother thought there would be two windows, so she made two pair of curtains."

Dad looked out the window. "At least you have one. Guess they figured the cowboy would like to watch the sun go down, so he'd know his day's work was over. He also could see anyone drive up." He turned to me. "Guess we'd better get busy and warm this place."

We lifted the stove from the truck and carried it to the center of the room. Dad connected a stovepipe and ran it up through the hole in the roof. He dumped a sack of coal and an armload of kindling into a wooden box. Soon he had a fire burning. I stood near it a moment before pitching in. The warmth felt good.

The old brass bed looked comfortable after I covered the well-worn mattress with sheets and two handmade comforters. The one made from worn out coats and corduroy pants was dark colored and of coarse material, so I put it on first. The top one had a design like a flower garden made from scraps of material left when Mother made dresses for her three girls.

While I worked, Dad went to inspect the spring. When he returned he said, "I'll bet this is a pretty place in the summer with those cottonwood trees all leafed out. That spring begins about half a mile from here. It's just seeping from the hillside. Been a long time since I've seen such clear water."

I paused in my search for enough nails on which to hang my dresses. "I wonder how old those trees are. Do you suppose they were planted? Or do you think some birds brought the seeds?"

"If I'm not mistaken, they were planted about fifty years ago. I've heard talk about this place. The fellows told me there used to be Fourth of July celebrations here that lasted for three days. Ranchers came from miles around to picnic and hold rodeos."

I smiled as I tried to visualize the festive occasion. "Wouldn't that have been fun? I wonder if they had fireworks?"

"I expect they did." He pulled a chair from the table and sat down as he watched me complete my tasks. "By the way, it looks as though you'll have

5

to use the Armstrong's backhouse. I don't see another one. It's on the right side of their yard."

I laughed. "That should be no problem. Just hope I can hook the door on the inside."

Dad stood and surveyed the room. "Guess you're about settled, so I'll go home. Hope you don't have any trouble finding the schoolhouse. There sure isn't a road that goes east."

"Don't worry. I'll find it. Mr. James said to go straight east until I saw a fence. Don't forget to come after me about five on Friday."

"I won't. Good luck on your first job," Dad said before he left. When he reached the truck, he turned and waved good-bye.

I walked back into my new home. I felt a little nervous so I began to hum. This was my first experience of spending a night alone. I was grateful for the curtain that could cover the window.

As I finished storing the kitchen supplies in a cupboard made from orange crates, I heard a knock on the door. I opened it to see a man and four boys.

"Howdy, Miss. My name's Armstrong and these is my sons fer you to learn. They're Larry, Bert, Albert, and Robert."

I shook his calloused hand. "Hello. I'm pleased to meet you." I noted he was about thirty, and all the boys resembled him. Robert had his sturdy build and Albert, his freckles. Bert's short hair stood on end like his father's and Larry had his delightful smile.

Mr. Armstrong said, "You can keep your milk, butter and meat in the springhouse outside your door. Guess you know you get your drinking water from the spring. If you need anything, let me know."

"Thank you very much. And thank you for cleaning the room."

"My wife done it. You kin meet her and our two little boys tomorrow." He and the boys started to leave.

"I'll look forward to that. Good-bye, boys. I'll see you in the morning."

After they left, I hummed again and wondered if I would remember which boy was which.

The glow of the sun no longer lighted the room, so I lit the gasoline lamp that sat on the table and pulled the curtain across the window. I didn't want any coyotes looking in. There was no key for the door, so I placed the back of one chair under the doorknob. Now I felt more secure.

A ham sandwich and glass of milk tasted good. As I reviewed my plans for the next morning, I ate an apple and read a short story in *The Saturday Evening Post*. Then, after I set the alarm for six o'clock, I had climbed into bed.

Now, the cowboy-shack school came closer and closer. I began to run while tears flooded my eyes. My adventure that had begun less than a week before led to that three mile walk to another beginning. This was the most exciting day of my life.

THE FIRST DAY

A tall dark complexioned man and two boys stood on the south side of the schoolhouse near the door.

"Good morning. I'm Miss Adams. I'm happy to see you."

The father removed an old felt hat. "Howdy, Miss. My name's Jackson. These is my boys. This is David, he's eleven." The man tucked his thumbs under the suspenders of his overalls. "And George will be eight next month."

I smiled at them. "Hello, boys." I noticed David resembled his father with his dark hair and eyes while George was blond with blue eyes. Both wore bib overalls, mackinaw jackets, and caps with worn visors that peaked in the center.

David grinned and looked up while George frowned and looked down. They stood close to their father as though they needed security.

"How long have you been here at the James ranch?"

"Two years, but we ain't had no school. I learned the boys all I could. I been tellin' Ennis we needed a teacher, but he wouldn't listen. Guess he changed his mind."

"I'm glad he did." I rubbed my hands together. "My fingers are so cold. Let's go inside so I can get the fire started."

"We already done it," David said as we entered. To my delight the pot-bellied stove in the middle of the room gave a welcome warmth. I held out my hands to absorb it.

The inside of the building didn't look any better than the unpainted wood siding on the exterior. The exposed rafters went up to the ridgepole and there was no covering of plaster or wallboard. I felt relieved there were no holes in the roof.

"Thank you for building the fire, Mr. Jackson."

The father seemed pleased at my reaction. "We brought some wood. Ennis bought coal, but forgot the wood. I'll try to bring more. You gotta have wood to start a fire."

I walked to my desk on the right side of the room and picked up a pail. "Did you bring this water bucket and dipper?"

The father, looking like a happy child who wanted recognition for his efforts, said, "Yep."

"It looks as though you thought of everything."

Mr. Jackson walked to the desk. "I'll do one more thing 'fore I go home. You'll get thirsty 'fore the day's over so I'll git this full of water."

He picked up the pail and started toward the door. "After today you better have the two older boys git the water 'fore school takes up. David and the oldest Armstrong boy can do that."

"Thank you for the suggestion. I'll discuss it with them. Where is the well?"

"It's at the windmill about a half mile from here. You kin see it the next time you go outdoors."

After he left I began to survey my surroundings. The six double desks of various sizes filled most of the area to the left of the stove. They faced the blackboard that was an eight foot piece of plaster board painted black. Except for a straight-backed chair near the desk the only other piece of furniture was a homemade bookshelf.

I had just hung my coat on a nail when the Armstrong boys arrived. They were beaming.

"Good morning." I tapped my temple. "Let's see if I remember your names and ages. Robert, you're eleven, Albert, you're eight."

"Nope. I'm nine. Bert's eight."

I nodded. "That's right. And Larry, you're seven."

He grinned. "Yep."

I turned to the Jackson boys. "Do you know them?"

"No," David said. "They live too far from us."

The six boys began to get acquainted as the newcomers took off their mackinaws. Robert looked at me. "I seed you, but I can't run as fast as you. In the morning I'll go with you. Pa sent this. He said we could use it in the backhouse." He handed me a Montgomery Ward catalogue.

"How thoughtful of your father." I opened it and tore it in half. "We'll keep part to use for towels in here."

I abandoned my planned schedule. The fire was already started and the room needed more than dusting. The dirt was so thick I couldn't see the floor.

"We need a scoop shovel more than a broom," I said as I began to push the dirt into piles. Albert followed me with the dust pan and carried the dirt outdoors. Robert and George moved the desks so I could sweep around them. David pulled a big rag from his pocket and began to tear it in half. "I'll use

8

part of this here 'kerchief for a duster." He stood looking at the desks, then laughed. "All we need is some water and we can make mud pies." He made some designs with his fingers before he brushed the dirt onto the floor. Bert and Larry watched the others as though they were supervisors.

When the room was clean the boys selected seats that fitted them best. I walked towards the bookshelf and asked, "Do any of you know what grade you're in?"

David and Robert thought they were fourth graders. The others didn't know. I devised a plan. As I stepped to the blackboard I said, "I'll put problems on the board. All of you start with the easiest ones and keep working as long as you can. While you're doing that I'll ask you one at a time to come to my desk and read."

The boys quietly followed my directions. Before recess I learned that Bert and Albert were second grade readers, and George and Larry would need the easiest books on the shelves. The two older boys struggled to read a Searson-Martin fourth reader.

During recess David and Robert gave a wrestling demonstration. The younger brothers counted to twenty as Robert held his opponent's shoulders on the ground.

"I'll bet I'm the fastest runner," Albert boasted. And he proved it by outrunning the other boys.

"Let's see who can win when we jump." Larry pulled me by the hand. "Will you try, Miss Adams?"

"Yes, but I expect David with his long legs will win."

With my heel I marked off the starting place across the dry grass. Each boy took his turn beginning with Larry who was the youngest. To my surprise I won. The boys clapped.

When we returned to the room I said, "Now I want you to write a letter to someone. Your grandparents would be pleased to hear you are in school."

"I don't write to nobody," Robert protested.

David shook his head. "Our grandpa ain't interested in us."

I didn't expect this kind of reaction so I thought fast. I needed to know how well they could express themselves in writing. "Then write to me. I'm interested in you. Tell me about today and what you think about me." There seemed to be a spark of interest in my request. "I won't read them until after supper. I'll answer every one of your letters. Doesn't that sound like fun?"

"I'll try," David said. The others nodded in agreement. All except Bert who asked if I would help him with spelling.

"Of course. I'll put any word on the board. Just write a few sentences."

Larry was the only one who didn't start.

"Can I help you?"

9

"What's a sentence?"

School hadn't been in session a half day and I was learning how limited these boys were. "Tell me about your dog."

"It's black."

"That's a sentence. When you tell something or ask something you make a sentence."

Larry sat, pencil in hand, looking at his paper and then at me. I walked to his desk and whispered, "Do you want some more help?"

Tears flooded his eyes. "Ya. I want to start with I, but I don't know how to spell it."

I patted his head and wrote the letter near the top of his paper.

"Oh," he said and began to write.

The other boys giggled. I shook my head and tapped my finger against my lips to quiet them.

During the next half hour I wrote several words on the board. After the letters were finished the boys put them in their desks to give to me after school.

Before lunch there was a knock. This surprised me as I did not expect more pupils or visitors. When I opened the door, a neat clean-shaven young man took off his Stetson hat and bowed. "Excuse me, Ma'am. I'm looking for Ennis. Do you know where I'll find him?"

"No, I have no idea. Maybe one of the boys can tell you." I turned toward the class. "Can any of you help this gentleman?"

Robert walked to the door. "He ain't no gentleman, he's Leo Feidler. He knows where to find Ennis."

Color flushed the visitor's cheeks. He cleared his throat. "That's right. I forgot." He twirled his hat on his finger. "Sorry to bother you, Miss. I'll be going now."

After I shut the door, Robert said, "Teacher, I think he wanted to know what you look like. He lives on the next ranch."

I felt my face getting hot. I wanted to say, "He's just a smart-alec," but pretended not to notice the boys' reaction as they put their heads down and raised their eyebrows and looked up at me. The older ones clamped their hands over their mouths.

When noon came I poured a dipper of water over each pupil's hands. We used paper from the catalogue for towels.

"We don't wash our hands at home 'fore we eat," Bert complained. " 'Sides, it's wasting water their pa brought."

I continued to pour the water. "You'll always wash your hands at school. My mother made us wash ours before we ate. Clean hands help to keep you well. I don't want you to get sick."

"We don't get sick," Bert said defiantly.

"That's good. Just remember it will be a school rule that you wash your hands before you eat lunch." The boys looked at each other as they decided I was the boss and there was no use to protest.

We sat at our desks to eat the cold lunches we'd brought. It was during this thirty minute period that I learned the two families lived seven miles from each other and there were no connecting roads.

When school was in session again I read an Aesop fable about the shepherd boy and the wolf. After I closed the book, David said, "That's a good story. Read some more."

I flipped swiftly through the book to find the poem "All Things Bright and Beautiful." It was a verse I had enjoyed for a long time. It told how God had made each little flower, each little bird, the purple-headed mountains, the morning and sunset and all the other wonders of nature. And it seemed to tell me that God would help to guide these six boys.

"I'll read more stories and poems tomorrow, but right now I want each of you to draw our flag. The school board should buy one so we can salute it each morning."

After a long discussion concerning how many stripes and stars and what they represented I said, "I'll divide the blackboard in six parts so each of you can practice drawing one."

"I can't."

"I don't know."

"I don't want to."

"I don't know how it looks."

"Now, now, I'll help you. Look at this one in the book."

Finally all the boys were at the board. None did a very good job, but all tried. When David finished he said, "I'll ask Pa if he'll make one. He makes our shirts."

"Your father does?" I asked in surprise. "Why doesn't your mother make them?"

He looked somber for a second. "She don't live with us. I ain't seen her since I was little."

"Ya, I was just a baby," George said.

I had an urge to hug both boys. "It would be wonderful if he could make a flag. Tell him we'll make the stars from paper and paste them on. Now all of you take your seats." I waited until they were quiet. "Tomorrow we'll talk more about our flag and our country. It's nearly time to go home. I wonder if we can sing a song we all know?"

There were no music books and none of them knew a patriotic song. David said his father had taught him the first verse of "Twenty Froggies Went to

School." After much coaxing he sang it. The boys snickered as they listened. I was happy to hear them clap when he finished.

Three-thirty came quickly that first afternoon. Before the children and I left we brought in a full bucket of coal and a few sticks of wood to start the fire next morning. As each boy handed me his letter I put it into my coat pocket.

When I returned to my shack I started the fire and prepared a supper of ham and beans. As I enjoyed the meal I reviewed my day with the pupils. I wondered if this school could be similar to those in the eighteen hundreds.

Perhaps the next time I attended Professor Wilson's history class at Chadron State Normal I could tell about my experiences here. He was a warm and knowledgeable man who brought our country's past into focus with clarity. He made me feel as though he knew personally everyone from Columbus to President Coolidge.

I recalled the previous summer when he had given us an assignment to write about some period in history. It was easier for me to talk than to write, so I decided to stay after class and ask the professor if he would give permission for me to present my assignment orally.

"What can I do for you, Miss Adams?"

"Would it be all right if I used a recent period in history for my assignment? I'm only eighteen, but I've lived history. I'm a pioneer."

"You are? He looked over his glasses and ran his fingers through his thick grey hair. Tell me about it."

"In 1914 my family homesteaded in Scotts Bluff County. We lived in a tent with gunny sacks on the ground for sixteen months until we built a sod house. We still live in the soddy. We have the certificate of ownership signed by President Woodrow Wilson that was issued in 1917.

"Of course today the 320 acres are worth much more than the $24.00 Dad paid in fees for the homestead, but that wasn't the price of the free land. The real price was the hardships we all endured."

He nodded. "I'd say you are a pioneer. What do you have in mind?"

"If I told the class about our experiences you wouldn't have to check my story for misspelled words or correct English."

He thought for a time, then said, "All right. That would be one less paper to correct." Professor Wilson shook his head and looked amazed. He waved his right hand toward the empty seats. "You'd rather stand up here and tell all those students about your experiences than write a report?"

I shrugged. "Sure. My friends say my hobby is talking."

He smiled. "Since you're so confident, shall we set a date for your talk?"

"Would next Friday fit into your schedule?" I asked.

He nodded, then picked up his date book and wrote in my name.

I was elated that he had agreed so readily to my suggestion.

Throughout the week I jotted down topics I thought would interest the class. Although I was only five at that time, I remembered how the pistols were shot that morning at nine o'clock to start the race for the land. Another was about the tornado that blew down a house near us, but killed only two of our hens.

That Friday as soon as the class was quiet and the roll was taken, Professor Wilson announced, "We have a pioneer in our midst and she is going to tell us about her experiences. Miss Adams, the floor is yours."

Although most of the students were older than I was, I didn't feel nervous. During my junior and senior years at Scottsbluff High School I'd been on debate teams, in a drama club and a public speaking class.

I had the subject so well in mind I didn't need my notes. I saw some shake their heads as though they couldn't believe our family had accomplished so much.

Most of them laughed when I told how Norman hung his stocking again the night after Christmas. The next morning he found it full of horse manure with a note attached to the stocking, "I had a pony for you, but it got away," signed, "Santa".

After I sat down I felt the class had enjoyed my talk because they applauded.

On my way to another class, a slender girl with short bobbed hair joined me.

"I'm Marie Sandoz. I'm Old Jules' daughter."

I wasn't impressed. I'd never heard of Old Jules. "My name is Treva, and my dad is Spud Adams."

She raised her eyebrows. "Everybody knows my dad. He's known all over the sandhills. He inspired farmers and ranchers in many ways. I might write about his life some day."

I still wasn't impressed. "Your father sounds interesting, but so is mine. My dad is known in five states because he takes the blue ribbons at all the potato shows. I like to brag about him to others, but that's as far as I'll go. I've never thought about writing. I'm going to be a teacher." When we reached the other classrooms we had said good-bye and parted.

Now, alone in my shack, I realized I had spent a good half hour recalling that day. I wondered if Marie Sandoz would really write about her dad.

Pushing aside memories of the past I decided it was time to read the boys' letters. A white glow from the gasoline lamp on the table lighted the room. With eager anticipation I unfolded them. Each started, "Dear Miss Adams."

David's was on top. It said: "I am glad you come us need a good teecher like you. I want to lrn you is purty. I like the way you laff and talk. Your dres looks good with your curly brown hair."

Larry's note was short and to the point: "I see you run I see you jump I see you walk fast. I like you." He didn't misspell any words.

Albert's note made me blush: "You is sweet. I like your brown iz. They git big sometimes. You sure can jump I think you is funny."

I was anxious to read George's letter. During the day I noticed his frown had often changed to a smile. "me like the way you talk and me like to here you laff and me will try to lrn to talk like you and me thank you for coming to us."

Bert's note made me feel special: "You is the best techer I has and you talk good and sum day I can be a techer like you and help kids to lrn. I luv you rite now."

When I read Robert's note I recalled that he had asked how to spell the most words. I noticed he used more periods than the others. "right now me don't know how to talk right but some day I will. You will help me. You is very special in this school because you learned us a lot today."

When I finished reading those dear letters, I didn't know whether to laugh or cry. They surely liked me and wanted to learn. In my notes I complimented them on their willingness to help clean the school, how it pleased me that they were polite to each other and wore neat clothes. In each note I wrote something that was not in any other.

It had been a long day. As I climbed into bed I thought about the things I had learned about those boys. I was so impressed with their desire to improve, the way they reacted to my suggestions, and their respect for each other. I knew it was going to be a good three months.

Carrying water to the first school at Wind Springs, 1928.

TEACHING AND LEARNING

The next morning Robert came to my door before I was ready to leave. He waited quietly until I put on my coat. "We, it, me like school," he said as we left.

It startled me to hear so many pronouns, but I smiled and said, "I'm happy to hear that. I know you want to learn so let's begin right now. It's better to say I like school."

"Pa, weren't sure what to use."

"He did the best he knew how. Now it's my turn to help."

He grinned. "Oh, guess I got a lot to do to git smart."

I patted him on the head. "Don't worry. The main thing is that you want to learn. You'll get better each day."

As we hurried along I considered how Mother had told me to stop using 'ain't'. I had waited until now to change that speech habit. But Robert's letter and this conversation indicated he wanted to improve right away.

"What do you want to do when you grow up?"

He glanced at me with a proud look. "I will be a cowboy like Pa. Only, I'm going to own a lot of cattle."

Before we'd walked the three miles I learned where he wanted to live and how many cattle he expected to own.

I hope all your dreams come true. My plans are to be the best teacher possible. Right now I hope we can start a fire in a hurry." I shook my fingers. "These mittens don't seem very warm. It must be freezing."

George and David arrived at school the same time we did. The three boys watched me crumple pages from the catalogue and place a few pieces of kindling on top before I lighted a match. When the wood began to crackle I shoveled in coal.

Before I took off my coat I laid on each boy's desk the letters I'd written. They had just begun to read them when the younger Armstrong boys arrived.

15

I saw smiles and shy glances at me and each other as they read. Only Larry asked for help to read his.

"You better go after the water," I told the two older boys. "Be careful not to spill it on your clothes. Why don't you find a long stick at the woodpile and put it through the bail? That way you'll each carry your share and won't have the bucket next to your legs."

They followed my suggestions and were soon on their way. Although David had already walked four miles and Robert three, neither complained about this extra mile. A tall windmill pumped water to keep the tank full for cattle. The boys would have to disconnect a pipe that carried water from the pump to the tank so they could fill their bucket.

It was nine o'clock when they returned. The boys took their seats to begin our second day together. Arithmetic was the first subject as it was considered the most difficult and children were more alert early in the morning. I soon found that the fathers had done their best teaching in that subject.

On Friday morning the Jackson brothers proudly brought the flag. The red and white colors were perfect. The blue field reminded me of the sky on a sunny summer day. It took a long time to make forty-eight five-pointed stars from construction paper. We tried to paste them on the flag, but when the paste dried the stars fell off. Finally we used a small brad to hold each in place. We hung the two by three foot banner near the blackboard. It not only brightened the room, but there was a feeling of pride and respect as we stood straight to salute our country's flag. We touched the edge of the right eyebrow and then extended our hands toward the flag as we said in unison:

"I pledge allegiance to the flag of the United States of
America and to the Republic for which it stands, one
Nation indivisible, with liberty and justice for all."

Silence filled the room. Then David said, "Now we have a real school."

The rest of the week passed quickly. On Friday when we left we were all looking forward to next Monday.

When Dad came that afternoon to take me home for the weekend, I bubbled over with stories about my first efforts as a teacher.

He said, "Don't wear yourself out on me. Your mother and sisters are anxious to know about it. Why don't you wait and tell all of us at the same time?"

"All right, if you insist. What happened at home this week?"

"Nothing much. It was pretty quiet without your chatter. I went to a couple of farm sales and Mom attended a meeting of the Women's Club. You know I always claim it's just a place to spread local gossip. Of course your mother told them about your new job."

When we drove into the yard, my sisters ran out to greet me. Eleven-year-old Helen said, "You don't look any different than you did before you became a school marm."

I stepped from the car and gave her a quick hug. Then she continued, "Did you spank anyone? Do you have any sixth graders?"

"What questions! I have six boys and the two oldest ones are struggling to be fourth graders. Robert tries to use all the pronouns in one sentence. He's getting down to one or two, but they are generally the wrong ones."

Dorothy picked up my suitcase. "Gee, I'd hate to teach such dumb kids." At thirteen, Dorothy, a tenth grader didn't seem aware that some children did not progress as fast as she did.

"They really aren't dumb. They all want to learn. Just give them time." I turned toward Helen. "The Jackson boys' haircuts are like yours. They have bangs. Their father does a pretty good job on the older one, but George looks as though his dad put a bowl over his head to use as a guide." The girls laughed, but I added, "The Armstrong boys look better. There are six of them so I guess their father has more experience. They are all towheads like you two."

When I reached the house Mother stood waiting in the open door. "We sure missed you," she said as we hugged. "Did you have enough food?"

"Yes, except milk. Guess I'd better take two gallons next week."

Before the weekend came to a close I had tried to answer everyone's questions. The girls were interested in the boys' letters. Dorothy said, "You must look kind of good to them."

Early Sunday afternoon Dad took me back to Wind Springs. He dropped me off and left. I barely had time to build a fire when Robert came to invite me to their house for cake. I put on my coat and went with him.

After I greeted the family I lifted six-month old Andrew into my arms and danced around the room and sang. When I sat down, he yelled as though a pin had stuck him. As soon as I stood he smiled, and when I began to move about he laughed. A few minutes later I again sat down. This time when he started his tantrums I handed him to his mother and said, "It appears Andrew is only going to like me when we're in motion. I guess I began something I may be sorry for."

Three-year-old Arthur leaned against my knees so I held him on my lap. He was as quiet as Bert. While I rocked the little boy I looked at his father whose appearance always seemed the same. His shirt didn't meet just above his belt, and his sandy colored hair appeared not to have been touched by a comb. He was proud to be a cowboy and talked about his profession. He told of his experiences as a bronco rider at rodeos when he was younger.

Rachael, his wife, a short roly-poly lady about thirty, seemed content to listen while her husband and I discussed many topics. I discovered she had attended school for only four years.

While we ate chocolate cake Roy Armstrong asked, "How come you didn't have a school when Ennis come to see you?"

I grinned and said, "It took me too long to learn to draw a fish."

He frowned. "What do you mean?"

"I planned to take a normal training class during my senior year of high school. It would have helped prepare me to become a teacher. Without it I had to study by myself to pass seventeen state tests pertaining to subjects and methods of teaching them."

"Why wasn't there a class?" he asked as he sipped coffee.

"Not enough students signed for it, so it was dropped."

"Did you have any trouble with the tests?"

I said, "By the time I graduated, I had passed all of them except art. On every drawing test the student was required to draw a fish." I paused and smiled. "I didn't want to admit I had missed other parts of the long test, so I blamed it on the fish."

He grinned. "That sounds like a good idea."

"I don't know about that, but in January I received a grade of ninety-six percent on my last attempt, so I applied for and received my certificate soon after."

Mrs. Armstrong came to the table. "Are you ready for more cake, Miss Adams?"

"No, thank you, but it is delicious and chocolate is my favorite."

Her husband wiped his mouth with his sleeve. "I could use another piece, Rachael." She gave him a second serving and returned to her rocking chair where she seemed satisfied to sit and listen.

I glanced at my watch and realized it was nearly nine o'clock. I stood to leave, but Mr. Armstrong wanted more information.

"Was passing tests all you needed to git your certificate?"

"No." I sat down again. "I attended the State Normal College at Chadron last summer where I earned twelve units. Now I can teach three years in grades one through eight."

Again I glanced at my watch, stood and put on my coat. Before I left he said, "The Mrs. and me is real pleased with what the boys is learnin'. I read with them last night."

"I'm happy to hear that."

Mrs. Armstrong added, "Us listen to what them say so us is learning with them."

"That's a good way to keep them inspired." I reached for the doorknob. "Thank you for a pleasant evening. Good night."

On my way home I thought about the couple and their use of the language. The whole family was learning and I was their teacher. I began to wonder how many lives I would influence throughout my teaching career. I hoped it would always be for the benefit of those I taught and met.

LESSONS FOR MISS ADAMS

One morning after school had been in session about six weeks, David and Robert returned from their usual one-half mile trip after water with only a half bucket full and out of breath. They set the pail near the door and began to relate their experiences.

Robert's eyes sparkled. "We saw about twenty antelopes."

David interrupted. "They stood on their hind legs with their front feet on the rim of the tank." He stopped to laugh. "They sure looked funny."

Now it was Robert's turn. "As they drank, their little bushy tails fanned the air."

Again David took over. "When they saw us they beat it. They ran with a hop just like jack rabbits. Their tails stick straight up." He demonstrated how they moved. Soon the four younger boys were mimicking him.

Robert rubbed his nose. "I'm thinkin'. If I had a rope I could catch one for a pet."

David shook his head. "Naw, they run too fast."

"Bet I could sneak up on them while they drink. I sure can lasso good."

"Brag, brag," Albert said.

David kicked the dirt with the toe of his shoe. "They ain't going to stay there. You saw how fast they run when we was a long way off."

"Yah, guess I'd better forget it, but I'd sure like to have one. I'd build a high fence so it couldn't git away."

Larry looked at his older brother. "You got good ideas, but this one won't work."

I watched and listened with great interest since I'd never seen an antelope and this was the first time the boys had shown a great deal of emotion about anything. "Have any of you seen one before?" None had. We decided the herd had come from the northern part of the county to graze on the new grass.

19

The boys recognized the animals from pictures. After that we saw the herd every morning.

We began to notice other indications of spring. Little purple jack-in-the-pulpits bloomed in protected areas, baby rabbits and ground squirrels scurried through the grass, insects buzzed over our heads, and cows nursed their calves.

A few days after we first saw the antelope, the boys came in from the afternoon recess smelling like a wild onion patch. The stink made me feel ill and I thought they had eaten the plants to upset me.

Without saying a word I left the room to find a narrow board at the woodpile and returned to spank the boys. Each bent over his desk to receive punishment like a gentleman. After I finished I became aware for the first time that they were pale. Soon they ran outdoors to vomit. Then it dawned on me they hadn't realized the effects of eating wild onions. I didn't think I needed to apologize for spanking them so I read stories and poems until nearly time for dismissal. By then they appeared to feel well.

I closed my book and said, "I've some extra work to do so I'll let you go now. Good night."

Not one offered to bring in coal and kindling or tell me good-bye.

When I was sure they were gone I covered my face with my hands and sobbed. I still had to sweep, dust, wash the blackboard and try to prepare lessons for the next day. Everything was an effort. Finally I closed the door and walked home. I didn't feel any better. It was a terrible evening and night. I kept wondering why I hadn't asked what made them eat those weeds.

None of the Armstrong boys walked to school with me the next morning. When they and the Jackson brothers arrived no one came in.

I picked up the pail and went out. "You boys had better go after the water. When you return we'll talk."

The four boys stayed outdoors until the brothers returned. After the six had taken their seats I began, "I'm sorry about yesterday. I thought you ate those onions to make me unhappy. When you became ill I knew you didn't know they'd make you sick."

David asked, "Why did you spank us?"

"Because I thought you should be punished for smelling up the classroom. Spanking was the way our parents punished us. It just seemed the right thing to do."

"That's the first time for me to get spanked," David volunteered. "Pa makes us sit on a chair for an hour without moving."

"Yah," George added, "and if we smile he adds ten minutes."

Bert raised his hand. "Ma makes me git on my knees and look at the wall. I can't talk when I'm there."

It was hard to believe gentle Bert would get into trouble. Then his brothers reported other forms of punishment in the Armstrong home, all considered "woman's work." They had to wash and dry dishes, make beds and sometimes even scrub the floors. As the boys talked they began to relax.

Albert had a serious look when he asked, "Miss Adams, will you tell us something bad you did to make your ma and pa spank you?"

I put the tips of my fingers over my mouth and thought. "I guess a similar example was when my brother and I drank vanilla." I made a face just remembering that experience. "Every time Mother used it we begged for some. She never gave us any, but said it didn't taste as good as it smelled. We didn't believe her so one day when she was gone, Norman swallowed a tablespoon of it. He smacked his lips as though he liked it and quickly poured some for me. I gulped it down. It tasted awful! I ran outdoors and vomited."

The boys smiled. "Just like us," they said almost in unison.

"That's right and as if we hadn't been punished enough our mother spanked us."

The boys nodded; "Just like us."

"Do you remember the last time *you* got spanked?" David asked.

"Yes, I'll never forget that. One day when our parents were gone, we three older children told Helen she was adopted because she had straight hair and ours was curly like Mother's.

"We teased her a lot because we thought Dad spoiled her. Maybe we were jealous of all the attention he gave her.

"When my dad heard her tearful story, he said she was the only one who belonged to him since his hair was straight too.

"That's when he spanked my brother, Dorothy and me."

"How old were you?" Larry wanted to know.

"I was twelve."

"Did you tease Helen again?" Robert asked.

"Oh, yes, but not about being adopted." I felt they were all happy once again so I said, "Let's get back to work. Shall we stand and repeat the pledge?"

A week later David found a small box turtle which he carried to school. This was a good introduction to a science lesson. We found a book with a picture and story about this dry land animal. We spent most of the day discussing different animals, their habitats, food and activities. This led to questions about the earth: "Where do we live? Do we live north or south of the equator?"

When I complained that we didn't have a globe, Robert said, "We got a big rubber ball at home. It's as big as my head. Can we make a world on it?"

"That's a good idea." I walked to the bookshelf and picked up an old geography book. "We can cut the continents from this and paste them on the ball. Why don't you ask your mother if we can use it?"

"Pa has the say. Ma does what Pa says."

"All right, then ask him."

The next morning Robert brought the ball and before the day was over we had a globe. Not only did it help us locate continents, but the boys used it to understand the cause for the changing of the seasons. They took turns representing the sun and earth. The boy holding the globe tipped it as he revolved around the "sun".

The globe was an aid in learning where various crops were grown. We discussed what we thought people ate. This led to our eating habits. David and George always had good lunches. The bread for sandwiches was made from whole wheat the father ground to make flour. They brought milk, hard boiled eggs, small jars filled with navy beans, apples and oranges.

We discussed balanced meals and why we should have them. The Armstrong brothers agreed it was a good idea, but their eating habits were foreign to it. Their lunches carried in old syrup pails bulged with apples, bananas and sandwiches filled with slices of meat the first couple of days after their father went to town. Then for the next two or three weeks they brought only four large pancakes with nothing on them. They never complained so I decided it was a custom they were used to. They appeared to be healthy and I figured there was nothing they could do to change their father's buying habits. I didn't stress nutrition again.

There was no playground equipment so the boys ran races, wrestled and played leap frog. One morning when the Armstrong brothers brought six turtles I suggested, "Put them in the coal box and we'll have a race at recess."

At ten-fifteen the boys made two circles in the dirt. After each claimed his animal and put a number on it with chalk, he placed it in the smaller circle. We waited and waited, but they stayed motionless with their heads hidden inside their shells.

When the fifteen minute play period was over David asked, "Can we do it again at noon?"

"If they're around. We must let them go now. They need to hunt for food."

Albert complained, "We don't have nothing to play with."

"I know," I said as we walked into the room, "and I'm sorry."

By noontime only one turtle could be found. The boys grumbled as they ate.

"Robert," I asked, "I saw an old car tire in your yard. Could you bring it? Maybe we can think of some games if we have several tires."

He clicked his tongue as though he thought that was a good idea. "I'll ask Pa."

David thought he could bring a rim to a wagon wheel and a car tire. The next morning the Armstrong boys brought two tires and a rubber tube they'd filled with a hand pump. David had a rim, but his father said the tire still could be used as a spare for the pick-up. Before nine the boys began to invent stunts and games with the discarded equipment.

They laid the tires and the tube side by side and hopped into each on the right foot. Then they competed to keep the tires rolling by using a stick. We couldn't think of a way to use the wagon rim. The activity they enjoyed most was racing the tire. I gave it a push, each boy in turn tried to run faster than the tire could roll within a given distance.

One day while we were eating lunch I said, "You have fun with junk and discards just as I did when I was your age. When I was eight Dad bought our first second-hand 1916 Dodge touring car for eight hundred dollars. He told Norman and me we could have our old buggy. We took the shaves off and pushed it to the top of the hill west of our house. We jumped in and took our chances as to where it would go. On the first trip the right wheel hit a large rock. As the buggy turned on its side we grabbed onto the frame that supported the top.

" 'Whew!' Norman exclaimed as we scrambled from the vehicle. It was a good thing the top was up, otherwise we'd probably been thrown out.

"I was too frightened to talk. As I crawled out I noticed my elbow was skinned. Norman took me to the horse tank where he washed the wound and used his blue handkerchief for a bandage.

"Before we took another ride we carefully scanned the area for large rocks. We used long sticks to dislodge them and rolled them down the hill. We used that buggy until one wheel came off."

"That's a good story. Will you tell another one?"

"Not today."

Later I told them another experience.

"One day I noticed Norman in the corral holding onto a cow's tail and having a merry time. Anything he did I thought I could do too, so I climbed through the barbed wire and grabbed a tail. The cow ran so fast I lost my balance. As I let go her tail I fell into the fence. I looked down to see blood pouring from a gash above my knee.

"I began to scream and cry. Norman rushed me to the horse tank. He washed away my tears, but he couldn't stop the flow of blood, so he wrapped his handkerchief around my leg.

"I limped to the house. When Mother saw the bandage she asked, 'What's that?'

I began to cry again. 'Don't whip him, don't whip him! He told me not to get hold of the cow's tail, but I wanted to do what he did.'

23

"She removed the handkerchief, cleaned the wound with turpentine, which she used for disinfectant, and bandaged it with a piece of old sheet.

"Mother shook her head. 'When will you ever learn you can't do everything your brother does? You'll probably carry a scar for life. I won't spank Norman, but your father will.' She put the turpentine away. 'Your brother has been told time and time again not to hold onto the cows' tails. This should be a good lesson for both of you.' "

George shook his head. "You got in trouble just like I do sometimes."

All the boys nodded in agreement. I wondered what they thought about their teacher getting into trouble.

I didn't tell them, but I remembered so well when Norman decided to brand a calf. He roped it and told me to hold the rope while he branded it.

He threw the calf to the ground and bound its fore legs together with a light cord. When the hot iron seared the animal's shoulder it bawled in agony, broke the cord and lunged to its feet. It began to run.

I didn't have sense enough to release the rope so as it tore through my hands it burned both of them. At first I felt no pain but later I could barely keep from crying.

During the next few days my palms festered and then scabs formed. Because it was too uncomfortable to keep my fingers straight during the healing period, my hands were cupped. I feared my hands would stay permanently in this position but my concern proved groundless.

It took nearly a month however, before I could grip the handle of the flat iron and help Mother with the ironing. I think that was the only time she didn't sympathize with my injuries. Maybe it was because she needed my help with that task and other household chores.

The students and I discussed many topics while we ate lunch. One day they talked about girls.

Robert said, "If they start, I won't come here."

"Me neither," the others chorused.

I asked, "What's the matter with girls?"

"They cry."

"They want their own way."

"They want to boss."

"They want to run everything."

"They want to be first."

"They don't like boys."

I shook my head. "How do you know? None of you have a sister and you haven't gone to school with girls."

Without hesitation, David said, "Pa says so."

Robert said, "Besides, we'd have to have another backhouse. It's all right for you to use ours, but we don't want no girls to use it."

I doubted that we'd have any girls in that school, so I didn't try to convince them that girls weren't as bad as they thought. I was learning when these boys were positive that they were right, I might as well not try to change them.

One afternoon just before dismissal Robert stepped to the door and yelled, "Look!"

We hurried to him and stood horrified as we watched a struggle between a pack of coyotes, a helpless calf and a few cows. The calf bleated in a high shrill voice. I yelled thinking I could frighten the coyotes away. The boys joined in. It did no good. We didn't dare leave the security of the school.

The mother cows lowered their heads and attempted to butt the coyotes. But they were driven back by bites on their noses and forelegs. Finally the cows backed away acknowledging defeat. We could see about a dozen beasts working as they tore the hide from the dead calf. It took only minutes for them to devour their meal and wander off.

We were so frightened that I wouldn't let George and David leave for home. It was nearly five when we saw their father coming. He was angry until he learned what had happened. After he saw the blood-stained grass and only a few pieces of bones and hide he said, "I guess you was smart to keep the boys here."

On the way home I admitted I had never had an experience like that before.

Bert asked, "Were you ever scared?"

"Yes, when I was fourteen."

He took my hand. "Will you tell us about it?"

"Well, every summer I herded cattle on the government preserve adjoining our ranch. There were about two hundred cows, yearlings, steers and one bull. They came from farms in the irrigated valley where there were no summer pastures. Dad charged one dollar a head per month for pasturing them.

"On this particular day I decided to ride Old Jim, our big white horse. The cattle had divided into two groups.

"Slowly I attempted to bring them closer together. I noticed the big red bull was in the herd I was moving. When I had ridden Nellie, the bay pony, I always had to be alert because he chased her, but had never bothered Old Jim.

"All of a sudden I felt myself sailing through the air. Luckily my feet had pulled free of the stirrups. Out of the corner of my eye I could see the bull's body, so I knew his head was under Old Jim's belly lifting him into the air. My head struck the ground with such force I was knocked unconscious. When I regained my senses I found my body was rolled up like a ball. My heart was beating rapidly and my head ached. I could see the bull pawing and snorting only a few feet away. Tears flooded my eyes, but I didn't make a sound.

"Suddenly the animal left to run after Old Jim who had put at least a half mile between himself and his attacker. The horse ran toward the house with his head high, so he wouldn't step on his dangling reins. Soon the bull gave up the chase and walked toward the herd.

"When I uncoiled my body I felt a great deal of pain in both shoulders. I cried all the way home. Tearfully I told my experience to the family.

"Dad said, 'You're lucky to be alive. If you'd moved, that bull could have trampled you to death.'

"Dad notified the owner to come after his animal. What a wonderful relief it was as I watched the bull leave."

I concluded by saying, "To this day if a bull comes within a hundred feet of me, I begin to shake and cry."

I looked at the boys. "I'm sure none of us will forget this day. I hope I never meet a pack of coyotes, or a bull, while walking to or from school."

Bert sighed. "I hope so too. I nearly cried this afternoon because I was so scared."

Larry added, "We'll always walk with you, Miss Adams. Wait 'til we tell our parents what happened. They'll be surprised."

"And so will mine," I said as we parted.

Six of the boys with the new playground equipment.

THE END OF THE FIRST TERM

One evening when I was at the Armstrong home, the father asked, "Will you teach our school another year?"

"Yes, if you want me. But we must have more supplies."

Mr. Armstrong shook his head. "Ennis won't like that. He's afeared his taxes will go up. That's the reason we ain't had no school these two years. I knew my boys needed a teacher, but this big house is important to me with a wife and six boys. I was afeared if I insisted there be school he'd fire me. I knew it were wrong, but I figured I could give my boys some learning." He looked sad as he drank coffee.

I leaned forward in my chair. "He must be a very wealthy man with this large ranch and hundreds of Hereford cattle. What will he do with all his money?"

Roy Armstrong sipped his coffee slowly. "I don't know. He's an old bachelor and never talks about his kin folks. You should see his little old sod house, and his truck looks worse than mine."

It was hard to believe he would defend this tightfisted miser. I wondered if there was another school in the whole country that had a homemade flag and a globe made from a rubber ball. And where else did children have to bring their own play equipment? If he and Mr. Jackson were afraid of Ennis, I wasn't.

"You sound as though you feel sorry for him. I'm sure he can afford a better house and truck." I rose to leave. "I don't care how he lives. I just want more supplies for this school." I looked at his wife who sat rocking little Andrew. "Good night, Mrs. Armstrong, I hope you agree with me."

She smiled. "I sure do. You come anytime. You give us something to think about."

With my hand on the door knob I looked at the father. "If you're afraid

27

to tell Ennis we need a decent amount of supplies and equipment, I'll tell him."

"Thanks, Miss Adams, guess I'd better tell him." He cleared his throat and grinned. "You might ruffle his feathers and us wouldn't git nothin'."

I chuckled. I decided he knew me well enough that I'd carry out my threat. "All right, good night." I left feeling I'd accomplished my mission.

One lunch time in the middle of May we watched a Ford touring car bounce over the prairie toward the school and stop near us.

Two clean-shaven young men jumped out and introduced themselves as salesman for *Bufton Universal Cyclopedia* published in Kansas City, Missouri.

"We have a real bargain for you," one said. "There are four volumes that cover many topics that we're sure you are teaching."

I asked, "How much are they? Let me see the first volume."

The boys crowded around me and the book that lay on the hood of the car.

"Pictures of dinosaurs!" David's voice reached a high pitch with excitement as I thumbed through the book.

"The set is seventy-five dollars, a real bargain. If you give us Twenty-five today you can have them. The rest you can pay off during the next two years."

I laughed. "How did you know I received a check last Friday?"

"We didn't, but we knew it was time for school to be out and you would be thinking about next year."

The second man interrupted, "There's a nice loose-leaf extension service you might like to take advantage of. Each year the company publishes an up-to-date volume of timely information. It includes a section for picture study and poems that are suitable for every month."

"That sounds interesting. How much more is that?"

"Twenty-five dollars each year and that will be available as long as you want it. You look as though you'd like the best for these boys. How about it, Miss?"

I did some quick thinking. Right then I had one hundred twenty-five dollars in the bank. Fifty dollars would be a sizeable amount, but in three weeks I'd get my final eighty dollars. I planned to return to Wind Springs and I knew these books would be a great help to the boys and future pupils.

I looked at my watch. "It's time for school to begin." Then I said to the boys, "Will you study real hard if I get them?"

"Yes, yes," they exclaimed in unison.

I turned back to the men. "Will you trust me? Leave the set and when I'm home Saturday I'll mail you a check."

The men stared at each other as though they were surprised I'd make such an offer. One explained, "This is the first time anyone has made such a proposition, but you look honest." He glanced at his partner. "What do you think, Al?"

"I really don't know what to say. I'll leave it up to you."

The first man said, "If we leave the books will you sign a statement that you'll send a check dated May 12, 1928 to our company for fifty dollars?"

"Sure. That's no problem. You write it out and I'll sign it after you put the four books on my desk."

The transaction was completed. The men left and the pupils and I spent most of the afternoon looking at the new books.

We held our last day of school picnic on the second of June. Both fathers had made an extra trip to buy food for the occasion. The lush green grass and large cottonwoods near my shack made a lovely setting for that special day. The boys waded in the creek and climbed trees until time for lunch.

As we gathered for the meal, Mr. Armstrong proudly announced he'd made lemonade for everyone.

David took a sip. "I don't think this is lemonade." He licked his lips. "It tastes like plain water."

Robert was defiant. "It 'tis too. I helped squeeze the lemons." He stuck his middle finger into his glass and pulled out a seed. He held it under David's nose. "What's this? It's a seed ain't it? Take a look."

David took another sip. "It still don't taste like lemonade. I'll have my pa make it next time."

"Huh," Robert scoffed, "go ahead, bet it won't be any better." He walked to the bucket to fill his glass again.

There was a variety of cold meats, bakery bread, apples, bananas and cookies. Mrs. Armstrong brought a chocolate cake.

Soon after lunch I passed out the report cards. Each boy yelled. "I passed! Thanks, Miss Adams."

They rushed to show their grades and my written comments to their parents. It was a happy time for everyone. Before the families left I gave each boy a hug and shook hands with his parents.

As I watched them leave I knew my first teaching experience had been successful. I probably had learned more than the students. There were times when I felt I was bumping my head against a brick wall, and other times when I watched progress far beyond my expectations. And their parents seemed satisfied. When I walked toward my shack, I thought, what more could I ask?

Now it was time to get ready for Dad's arrival. He would be there at five and he didn't like to wait. When I saw a cloud of dust streaking across the prairie, I knew it was Dad. He thought getting from 'here to there' was a waste of time. Before we had a car he always said if anyone went over twenty-five miles an hour he would be a darn fool, but after he bought our first car, the family said the only time he went under that was when he started and stopped.

29

This was typical of him, always on the go. Perhaps that's why he was so physically fit, all muscle. His eyes sparkled when he smiled. We seldom saw him laugh, but when he did it was a hearty one. My friends often told me I sounded like Dad when I was amused.

He brought the Dodge to a quick stop, jumped out, slammed the door, and strode to my shack. "Hi, I'll make my usual inspection of the spring while you load your things." And off he went. He never interfered with duties that he considered 'woman's work' so I didn't anticipate or receive any help when I carried my clothes, bedding, and cooking utensils to the car.

We had just started homeward on the narrow dusty one-lane road when Dad said, "I'm sure glad you don't expect to attend college this summer. I've made a big deal with Eben Warner, and I'll need you."

"What does Mr. Warner have to do with me? He owns the telephone company and I'm a teacher."

Dad waited a few minutes before he answered. "He's decided to branch out by starting a big industry in the valley. He's going to build several cheese factories."

I interrupted. "I don't see how this involves me."

Dad's voice trembled with excitement. "Just hold your horses and I'll get to you. Right now a young fellow is in Wisconsin buying dairy cows to sell to local farmers. The first hundred head will be here next week. We're to pasture them until they're sold."

I nodded. "Now I know why you're glad I'll be home. You expect me to herd them."

It was a good thing I had no definite plans for the summer. I hadn't earned enough salary those three months so I could attend college. Now Dad took care of my time.

"That's right." His eyes squinted. "We're farming too much acreage for me to do it alone. Although Norman will be home next week he can't take on more responsibility. Your sisters will help you. Before the summer's over Eben said we'll have about five hundred cows coming and going. Of course he hopes to sell all of them by the first of September."

I surprised myself by having the nerve to ask, "Is it a free board and room deal like it's always been, or do I get wages now that I'm a school marm?"

Dad was quiet for a few minutes, then said, "Let's make a deal. If you'll herd all summer, I'll put a seventy-five dollar payment on a car. You need one."

"That's right. I told the pupils I'd be back in September. I don't want you to continue to take me on weekends."

Dad continued, "I've been asking around. You can get a pretty good second hand Model-T for two hundred dollars. You can pay off the rest in monthly payments of fifteen or twenty dollars."

I wanted to snicker. Dad was helping me spend my next year's salary. I was sure he knew he was making a good deal for himself. For the past ten years pasturing cattle that belonged to farmers had been one source for our family's income. I'd herded cattle since I was eight except for last summer when I attended college.

By the time we finished this conversation we'd gone twenty miles and had driven through the third cattle guard. For the next ten miles we traveled on a well graded road at about thirty-five miles per hour. Then we left this main thoroughfare to reach our ranch. Dad didn't slow down. He knew every twist and turn, and held firmly to the steering wheel. It was up to me to brace my feet and hold on to the dashboard to keep my balance. As we bumped along I planned that one of the first things I'd do after I had my car was to take Dad for a fast ride to give him a good taste of his own medicine.

When we drove into the yard and stopped he blew the horn. The girls ran out to meet us. Dad pushed his straw hat back and said, "You didn't talk much coming home. What did you think?"

"I think you won, just like you always do." I wondered when I'd be in charge of my life. Maybe I was still fortunate because I'd heard Dad say his parents took part of their children's salaries as long as they lived at home.

He smiled and walked toward the house while my sisters and I carried my possessions from the back seat to the bedroom and kitchen.

Treva Adams at age 19 during the summer of 1928.

HENRY

On the following Tuesday big trucks delivered the Holstein and Brown Swiss cows. The animals looked tired after their long trip by train from Wisconsin to Scottsbluff, twelve miles south of our ranch. Most of them were big with calf and moved slowly.

I spent the first day keeping the herd together and helping them find the best places to reach water at Lake Alice, a storage reservoir that belonged to the Pathfinder Irrigation District.

This artificial body of water about a mile long and three-fourths of a mile wide, was confined by two earthen dams that had been built in 1912 on U.S. government land. Dad was permitted to pasture cattle around the lake providing they didn't get on the dams.

Herding them was a long, hot, boring twelve-hour-a-day job. I seldom saw friends, but on weekends families traveled the one-lane road around the lake to fish and swim.

Every morning I dressed in bib overalls and a man's blue shirt. Although the clothes were hot when the temperature went over a hundred degrees, the long sleeves, high collar and pant legs protected me from the intense rays of the sun. My face and hands tanned until friends asked, "To which tribe of Indians do you belong?"

After I opened the corral gate at six in the morning the cattle grazed toward the lake. This gave me time to help Mother, prepare my lunch, and select a magazine or book to help pass the hours. Then I bridled Nellie, our bay mare, and headed toward the herd. There was no need for a saddle because her rounded body served as a cushion.

This was a hum-drum everyday routine until one morning, just as I was going to leave the house, Helen and Dorothy came running in laughing so hard Mother and I could hardly understand their words.

"There's the funniest man down at the corral," Helen said. "His name's Henry. He doesn't talk like we do."

I frowned. "What do you mean?"

"He says 'mit' instead of with and 'dink' instead of think."

Dorothy added, "Guess he can't pronounce 'th.' He also can't sound 'w' because he said 'vant' for want and 'vait' for wait. You'd better hurry, Sis, so you can see him. You might get yourself a new beau."

I hurried, but luck was not with me. The "funny man" drove away in his Ford just as I put the bridle on Nellie.

That evening my sisters entertained the family with stories about Henry as we ate supper. He had told them he could ride a bicycle, but not a horse, and he did tricks with his stiff-rimmed straw hat. He smoked a stub of a cigar in his pipe. When the girls asked why, he said that he followed the healthy men down the street until they threw away their cigars. These were what he smoked.

Cautiously I asked, "How does he look?"

Helen laughed. "He's just kinda big and he puts his finger beside his nose when he talks too fast 'cause he stutters."

Dad stopped eating. "That's because our language still bothers him. He's a native of Holland where he learned to be a veterinarian. He knows a lot about the dairy industry."

Norman, who had just returned from university, said, "Holland's educational system has a fine reputation for being advanced and thorough. He's probably well qualified to perform any duties Mr. Warner has for him."

This discussion whetted my desire to meet Henry. My opportunity came the next afternoon when I watched two young men in a new sports car with a rumble seat bounce over the prairie toward me.

When they stopped nearby, a heavy-set, blond, blue-eyed fellow called, "Miss Adams, I'm Henry Ottjes. I work for Mr. Warner. He's at the corral. He wants to see the cattle. We must take them right in."

He spoke with an accent, just as my sisters had described. Nellie continued to graze and I didn't bother her.

"We must hurry, Miss Adams."

I looked at my watch. "It's only one o'clock. Dad told me to keep the cattle out until six." I didn't really like a conflict with Henry the first time we met, but I felt Dad's instructions should be followed. "If Mr. Warner wants to see them he'd better come here."

"But Mr. Warner said he wants them in the corral." His voice indicated a trace of anger.

I shrugged. "Dad is my boss, so you and your buddy in his fancy car better get busy and get them there."

The driver moved closer. "What's the matter, Henry?"

"She said her father told her to keep the cattle here until six. Guess it's up to us to take them to the corral. Miss Adams, this is Bill Cook. His father owns the packing plant."

"You're putting us in a terrible predicament," Bill said. "My Dad and Mr. Warner are waiting for us to bring the cattle."

"Then you'd better get busy."

Bill blew the car horn and Henry ran here and there trying to get the cattle into a bunch. Nellie and I followed the straggling herd. When the cattle were near the corral I hurried to the house.

That evening Dad smiled as he said, "I noticed you had plenty of help getting the cattle in the corral. It appeared your helpers did more work than you. I heard them grumbling to Eben about it."

I looked straight at Dad. "I was just following your orders." I had mixed feelings whether or not I'd done the right thing, but continued to defend myself. "If Mr. Warner wanted to see the cattle it seemed more sensible for him to come where they were." This could become a habit that I wanted stopped before it got started.

Dad nodded. "Guess you made your point. I overheard Eben say next time they'll either come early in the morning or after six."

Dorothy punched my elbow. "Bet you'll never get a date now. I was wishing for a little romance and excitement around here."

"Oh, be quiet! I hate to be bossed. At least Henry knows something about my idea of following instructions."

Helen snickered. "Ha, he'll probably think you're pretty stubborn."

Mother came to my defense. "I can see Treva's point. It would have been more sensible for those two men to drive to where the cattle were."

Dad closed the discussion. "Well, what's done is done. Let's change the subject."

About a week later Henry drove his car close to where I sat on Nellie who was grazing. He asked politely if I'd noticed any cattle that showed signs of illness, then he walked slowly among the herd. New calves appeared nearly every day so Henry came often from then on. Sometimes he brought prospective buyers for the animals. He was always courteous and made it a point to speak to me. I felt he'd forgiven me for my rudeness the first time we met and I looked forward to his visits.

After several trips he began to relax. One morning he edged closer and patted Nellie's neck. "She's a good horse."

"Yes, I prefer her to Old Jim. When I ride him I have to use a saddle."

Henry continued to stroke the horse. "What else do you do with your time?"

I raised my eyebrows and tried to keep my voice normal. "I don't have much leisure, but occasionally a bunch of us attend the movie."

"Do you like carnivals?" He paused as though watching my facial expression to know how to proceed. "There is one in Scottsbluff. Would you like to go with me Saturday night?"

My heart quickened. I really wanted to know Henry better, but I had mixed feelings about being seen with him. I'd never dated anyone who had been born in a foreign country and spoke with an accent. What would my friends think?

I stalled. "I'll have to ask Dad. He's very particular about my dates. I'll let you know in a couple of days."

He didn't seem disturbed. Perhaps this was a custom familiar to him in Holland. His expression was warm and friendly. "That's all right. You can tell me when I come again."

For the first time I told him good-bye. He smiled. "I'll see you soon." He hurried to his car, tipped his hat and left.

That afternoon four friends came to visit. I learned the boys knew Henry and liked him. They enjoyed his wit. The girls seemed interested, so I decided to accept Henry's invitation.

I looked forward to Saturday with greater anticipation than I had with other dates. I wondered what we would talk about. Would he tell jokes to me like he did to my sisters? Should I ask him about his family? Would he be easy to converse with?

By Saturday Helen and Dorothy seemed excited too. "Are you going to wear your overalls so he'll know you?" Helen asked.

"Don't be funny. I'm wearing the dress I bought with my first check." While the girls watched I took it from the closet. "He hasn't seen me in a dress. Maybe he doesn't know I'm a girl."

Dorothy laughed. "Ha, he knows all right. Anytime he comes and doesn't see you, he wants to know what you're doing."

It was nice to know he'd been interested in me for some time. I hoped he'd continue to be after our first date.

Later that day while I was dressing, Helen came in. "Tell us in the morning which rides you like best. Daddy's promised to take us next Saturday." She stood for a few minutes in silence.

"But I wish we could go tonight." She sat on the bed and swung her legs over the edge. "I'd follow you to see if Henry holds your hand."

I gave her a stern look. "I'm glad you're not going. I'm sure both of you would give me a bad time. I promise to give a full report."

"Full?" Dorothy asked as she walked into the room.

"Yes, full." I shook my finger at the girls. "You two better behave when he comes."

A half hour later Henry drove into the yard. We three watched through the window as he walked to the corral where Mother was milking the cows.

"Maybe he's forgotten who he has a date with," Dorothy said.

This remark set us giggling. When I opened the door I had a difficult time stifling my laughter. I could hear the girls snickering as we left.

Henry looked very handsome in a light blue suit that fitted him well. It was the first time I'd seen him without a hat. I noticed his blond hair was a bit thin on top. "You sure look nice," I greeted him. He took my hand and smiled. "The color of your suit matches your eyes."

He bowed. "Thank you. And this is the first time I've seen you in a dress. Pink is a good color for you."

Under the watchful eyes of my sisters we walked to his car. He opened the door on the passenger's side. I stepped on the running board as he held my arm. When I was seated he closed the door. This was a new experience for me as my other beaus didn't extend this courtesy so I felt very special.

On the way to the carnival he asked, "What do you enjoy most?"

"I like the rides and sideshows although they seem to get more expensive each year. We used to pay just a nickel for rides and a dime to watch animals perform." I laughed. "Once a classmate paid two and a half dollars for each of us to watch a boxing match. I thought he was a millionaire!"

Henry's mouth quirked in a humorous line. "How did he get the money?"

"His dad made hooch. Guess you know that's liquor. The still was in the area of my school in Sioux County. Bill and his sister were the best dressed kids at Lake Alice School."

Henry looked puzzled. "Why would you want to watch a boxing match?"

I gave a palm up gesture. "Perhaps because I've boxed since I was twelve."

"You box?"

"Yes. Once Norman came home with a black eye after he and a friend fought over a girl. Dad decided Norman should learn to handle his hands better. He needed a boxing partner and I was it."

Henry leaned over to look at my face. "Are you kidding?" He nearly ran off the road.

"No. I got pretty good. In fact when I was fourteen I knocked out a boy three years older than I."

Henry shook his head in disbelief.

"I wasn't supposed to box with anyone except Norman. It was during the noon hour while the folks rested that I slipped into the house, grabbed the gloves and took them to the spud cellar."

"Who was the victim?"

"An orphan kid who lived with us. He challenged me." I shrugged. "So what else could I do?"

37

I laughed thinking about it. "First I hit him on top of his head and then on his chest. That knocked the wind out of him so he fell to the ground unconscious."

Again I paused to recall that incident. "Was I ever scared! I ran to the house yelling, 'I killed him, I killed him!' By the time the family entered the cellar he was sitting up, looking rather pale."

Slowly Henry shook his head. He drove nearly a mile before he spoke. "Well, I'll be on the watch. For sure we will not attend a prize fight or boxing match tonight. I think we'll just take rides."

"That suits me."

Soon we reached the carnival where we had a delightful evening riding on every movable device including a new one called "The Caterpillar." The green colored worm with seats for twenty passengers traveled on a track shaped in a figure eight. As soon as we were in motion a hood covered us so we were in complete darkness. I could hear many squeals and shrieks as we went around curves. Apparently all of us were having difficulty staying in our seats.

When eleven o'clock arrived I said, "I'll be going up and down in my sleep tonight. I've had enough rides for one time, haven't you?"

"Ya, I think so."

It had been a good evening and I hoped he would ask me to go out with him again. On the way home he did.

"Would you like to see my farm? I just had all the buildings painted white and trimmed with red."

"I didn't know you had a farm. Where is it and how long have you had it?"

"I just bought it last year and it's in Sunflower community about twelve miles from here. In Holland I could never have one. They are handed down from father to son so they are never sold. Now I have what I want most. Do you think you could go tomorrow?"

"Yes, if I can talk my sisters into watching the cattle. Come about two. I'll try to be ready."

When we arrived home he escorted me to the door and shook my hand. "Thank you for going with me tonight."

I beamed. "Thank you for asking me. I had a very good time. Good night."

The moon shone through the window so I undressed and got into bed without lighting a lamp. It had been such an enjoyable evening I had a difficult time falling asleep.

The next morning I tried to answer everyone's questions. The girls agreed to watch the cattle that afternoon.

When Henry came he stopped to chat with Dad who sat in the shade of a tree reading a magazine. I joined them for a short time and then Henry and I left.

The two hundred and forty acre farm had well-kept buildings. Near the road a herd of Holsteins was lying in the shade of a large grove of cotton woods. I pointed toward them. "That's one of the prettiest groves I've ever seen."

"Ya, those trees made me want to buy this place. Someday I will plant more trees."

We strolled behind the barns where a large meadow had a drainage ditch running through it. Beyond were fields of corn, pinto beans and alfalfa. Farther north was dry land pasture.

As we walked toward the car I said, "You surely have a fine investment."

"I think so and it didn't cost too much. I bought it at a foreclosure sale. I felt sorry for the man who lost it because he could no longer make his payments. I paid two thousand dollars."

"This depression is hard on many. The house looks nice. How many rooms does it have?"

"Two upstairs and three down. I didn't pay much attention. The farm buildings interested me most."

As we drove away I asked, "Do you think you'll live here sometime?"

"Ya, if I get married."

From then on for the rest of the summer I had a date with Henry every Saturday evening and sometimes on Sunday afternoon.

Henry Ottjes

THE SECOND TERM

In the middle of August Ennis came to have me sign a contract for the next nine months with a week off for Christmas, Thanksgiving Day and New Year's Day. My salary would be seventy-five dollars for each twenty days. I was so content to have full employment the amount of money seemed immaterial.

Before he left I handed him a list of books and supplies. He frowned as he read it. "I don't want my taxes raised so I'll decide what's necessary."

I straightened my shoulders and lifted my chin. "We need everything on that list."

He glanced at it again and stuck it in his vest pocket. "I'll see what I can do. It looks pretty long. Good-bye. I'll see you next month."

Everything was set for a good year. I had a contract and felt Ennis would buy most if not all the items on the list. I'd learned so much last spring. Now I was ready to be the best teacher any pupil ever had. I knew I wouldn't spank those boys again if they ate a whole acre of wild onions. I still felt chagrined that I'd done it.

Soon after I'd signed my contract Dad came home with a black, Model-T coupe. I recalled Henry Ford once said, "You can have any color you want just so it's black." The car cost two hundred-fifty dollars. Dad put seventy-five dollars down and I would pay off the rest in fifteen dollars a month payments. Two adults could sit comfortably on the narrow seat.

I'd learned to drive our Dodge when I was twelve, so steering was no problem. Mother refused to learn to drive at that time, and often Dad or Norman couldn't take her to Sunday School. It was held at Lake Alice school over four miles away.

Our garage was just wide enough for the car and space for the driver to enter or exit it. Any passengers had to get in or out before the car was driven into the building.

Dad said, "It's easy for anyone to learn to drive in, but I think it's also important to learn to back up, so Treva, when you can back into the garage you're ready to drive."

I can't remember how often I'd torn the doors from the garage when I backed up. Dad never scolded. He just fastened them on again and kept encouraging me.

How proud I was when I took Mother and my sisters to Sunday School that first time. I wanted to tell everyone, but we'd just arrived in time to hear Mrs. Lemley, the superintendent of the Sunday School announce, "It's time to start. I notice Mrs. Adams, and her daughters finally got here. I wonder what Mrs. Lutton's excuse will be that she's not here? I'm baking bread and the dough may be on the floor when I get home, but I'm here where I belong."

Sunday School meant a great deal to my brother and me and it was about the only time we saw our friends. Before he or I could drive a car we rode our horses to the services.

Dad's voice, telling me how to start the engine brought my mind back to the task at hand. He pointed to the shaft holding the steering wheel. "Notice those two levers just a few inches below the wheel? The one on the right is the gas. You'll soon learn how much you need to get the engine going, but not flooded. The one on the left is the spark. Too many careless persons have broken their arms when they'd crank and the engine kicked. As soon a the engine hums, hurry to pull down both levers."

"Why do I have to learn to crank? There's a self-starter."

Dad shook his head. "You can't depend on it. Most of the time it won't start the engine. I don't want you stuck out on the prairie somewhere not knowing how to crank this flivver."

He instructed me in the use of the three foot pedals. The right one was the brake, reverse was in the middle, and the left one was the clutch. Speed was regulated by adjusting and readjusting the gas lever.

It took nearly a week of practice driving near home before I ventured onto the public road. By then it was time to think more about school.

I decided to improve the appearance of my shack by following Mother's method of spring cleaning, so I looked at her Montgomery Ward wallpaper catalogue to order bright yellow paper.

After it came in the mail I left for Wind Springs Ranch the next morning at five o'clock.

It was an uneventful trip until I came to the third and last cattle guard before reaching the ranch. I brought my car to an abrupt stop when I saw ropes stretched above the guard. Upon closer observation I noticed broken pipes in the crossing. This meant I'd have to open the big wire gate beside the guard. When I started to pull the stake from the lower wire loop, my eyes opened wide. There lay a ten dollar bill. This would purchase a four week supply of groceries to supplement the vegetables from the garden. "Thank you, whoever you are." I stuck the money into a pocket of my overalls, drove through the gate, fastened it and was on my way.

When I drove into the yard at the ranch, the boys ran out to greet me.

"Miss Adams," Robert hopped on one foot and then the other. "You can't guess what we have for a pet."

"No, did you get a new dog?"

The boys shook their heads. "Nope," Robert continued, "It's a baby coyote."

Albert added. "Pa makes us keep it penned up so it won't eat the chickens. You gotta see it. Hurry."

"All right, just as soon as I take these things in and put them on the table. I'm going to paper my home today."

The boys helped me carry the paper, scissors, yard stick, rags, and pan of homemade paste. We laid everything down and hurried toward the pen.

"We found three babies in a den. They were so cute," Albert said with a smile, then frowned. "Pa killed two of 'em 'cause he said they'd just grow up to kill calves."

Larry interrupted, "Hurry, Miss Adams." He grabbed my hand to pull me along. "You can pet Charley. He won't hurt you."

When we reached the pen, Bert jumped in. The animal looked content as he followed the boy around the enclosure.

"What do you feed him? He looks fat."

Robert shrugged, "Pancakes, or anything left on the table."

I reached over the woven wire fence and petted Charley on the head. His beady eyes stared at me. He seemed as gentle as a puppy. I gave him a final pat and said, "Good-bye, I've got to get busy." I said to the boys, "I think you can write some good stories about Charley this fall."

Because they had so few pleasures I didn't tell them about the time when Norman was twelve and he found a new-born coyote and brought it home.

Dad warned it would kill chickens, but we children didn't believe him. We gave the baby coyote so much attention that our dog, Roger seemed jealous, but accepted Tag-a-long as a playmate. They ate and slept together in a crude doghouse Norman had made.

One morning when the coyote was about three months old, Mother found a dead chicken with no evidence of how it had died. The next morning, she discovered two more dead. Before the afternoon was over Tag-a-long was seen catching a Leghorn hen.

"That's it!" Dad exclaimed. "I told you this would happen. Norman, get your twenty-two, have that pesky animal follow you to the hill and don't shed any tears around me."

We children did cry and Mother seemed to be sad, but Dad never let on he was sorry the culprit was dead.

Now, watching the Armstrong children as they ran toward their house I hoped their new pet, Charley, wouldn't suffer the same fate as our Tag-a-long. I put the problem from my mind and hurried to my shack.

I worked fast, but carefully, so by four that afternoon my shack looked beautiful with the walls covered with the new wallpaper. I hurried home to brag about my accomplishments and finding that money.

From then on I counted the days until school would start. My Model-T was really loaded as I left for the ranch the last Sunday in August.

When I drove into the yard the boys came to help me unload. Robert greeted me with, "Ennis brought a lot of boxes. They're in our house. When can we open them?"

"In the morning at school. I'm as anxious as you to learn what he brought, but it's best we wait so the other boys can enjoy opening them as well." They looked disappointed but didn't argue.

After I put everything in place I went with the boys to their home. Mr. and Mrs. Armstrong greeted me as the two little boys hugged my legs.

The boxes were in the living room near the door. The father and the boys carried them to my car and put them in the trunk. "Let the boys help unload these. They're heavy."

Later, I opened a small package from the County Superintendent's office and found a registry, monthly attendance cards and a dozen report cards.

Next morning the boys smiled broadly as they climbed into my Ford. Albert, Robert and Bert sat beside me while Larry sat on Albert's lap. We took the main road south for three miles, turned east to cross Wind Springs Creek and followed a lane for another four miles. We were in the middle of the creek when the door opened on the passenger side and Robert fell into the water.

"Stop, stop!" Albert yelled as though I were a mile away.

I stepped on the brake, then realized I needed to get through the creek before I stopped so I drove on. I slammed on the brakes again. The boys and I hurried to the water's edge. Robert, with a sheepish grin and soaking wet, waded from the stream.

"Did you open the door? I didn't know you were thirsty."

"No. I didn't do nothin'."

"It doesn't matter, you aren't hurt. That's the main thing. You better take off your outer clothes and lay them on the ledge behind us. When you get in be sure to close the door tight."

He didn't move. Albert urged. "Come on, hurry up. Do what she says."

Robert asked, "Do I have to?" He looked embarrassed.

"I believe your clothes will dry quicker and you won't get Bert wet beside you."

I turned toward the car.

"She won't look at you," Albert assured him.

Robert slowly walked behind the car, removed his clothes and threw them onto the ledge, then he climbed in.

Convincingly I said, "They'll be dry before nine o'clock." I started the engine and we resumed our bumpy ride.

When the school came into view we saw a touring car parked near the door. Just as we approached a lady and three girls emerged.

"Gee, who are they?" asked Larry.

"Girls, can't you see," Bert said in a matter-of-fact voice.

"Ya, girls," Robert and Albert echoed in unison and turned up their noses as though they'd practiced their act.

At last I had girls! Again without looking at Robert I said, "Stay here until the girls and their mother are inside." I reached back and felt the clothes. "They're nearly dry. As warm as it is you won't catch cold if you put them on now."

I stepped from the car to greet the newcomers. "Good morning, I'm Miss Adams." I shook the lady's hand. "I'm so pleased you brought us some girls. We really need them."

Mrs. Lockwood introduced herself, Rachel, Ruth and Carol, as I pushed open the door. All three girls had blue eyes and blond curls. They wore fancy, homemade organdy dresses and long white cotton stockings and black shoes.

"We just moved onto the Elwood Ranch," the mother explained as she glanced around the room. "This is our closest school and we're eight miles away."

I shook my head. "You're driving thirty-two miles a day! I walk three miles across the prairie, but this morning I drove to bring supplies." I paused and scanned the scene before me. Dust coated everything. "Please excuse me. I have many things to do so I'd better get busy." I looked at the girls. "Wait until I dust the desks, then you may select any one you think will fit you best."

As the mother moved toward the door I said, "School will be dismissed at three-thirty. We have a half hour noon recess."

Mrs. Lockwood spoke to her daughters. "You help Miss Adams and I'll see you this afternoon." She gave little Carol a hug, returned to her car and drove away.

Soon after the mother left, George and David arrived. The boys came to the door, looked in and then disappeared. I carried the waterbucket outside to find the boys huddled around Robert. I didn't know whether to scold or

45

sympathize. Their kingdom had been invaded. I began by saying, "Aren't the girls pretty?"

The boys frowned, raised their eyebrows, made funny faces and sneered.

I looked at the older ones. "You'd better go after the water." David took the bucket reluctantly. "Robert, your clothes will be dry by the time you return." He kicked a small bush with the toe of his shoe and followed David.

"Now will you other boys help me unload the car? We should have a flag and a globe."

They didn't budge.

"Oh, come on," I coaxed. "Those girls won't bite you. Don't you want to know what's in the boxes?" I paused wondering how I could change their mood. "If you're worried about the backhouse the girls will use it during school time. It's yours at noon and recess."

This seemed to ease their minds. They followed me to the car, carried the boxes inside and shyly greeted the girls. When the older boys returned with the water, we started to open the boxes. Soon all were busy. George grabbed the long narrow cardboard box first. He used a screw driver I'd brought to open one end, and out slid a beautiful flag with forty-eight stars on a field of blue. He held it up, "It sure looks different than the one we had last year."

"That's true," I agreed, "But don't forget we'll always remember our homemade one."

Everyone stopped to watch me drive two long nails into the edge of the blackboard. I then bent them over with my hammer to hold the flag in place.

"It's a real school now," Larry said and gave a quick salute.

Albert returned to his task of opening the box marked "globe." When he held the ball in his hands he whirled it round and round. "Is Wind Springs on this?"

"No. Find the boundary between Wyoming and Nebraska and you'll know where we live."

The boys stopped to look at Albert, but the girls were more interested in the reading books. Bert found a science text that had pictures of dinosaurs. The girls joined the boys to look for a few minutes. Carol said. "Those big animals aren't pretty."

The largest box was the last to be opened. It contained a long and short jump rope, two baseball bats, three hard balls, and a large one that could be used to kick or throw.

Albert was the first to express his elation. "This is great. Can we take them right now and try them out?"

"Of course. That's what they're for."

After the boys left the girls helped me stack the books on the shelves. I was pleased to find Ennis had bought two small dictionaries.

When it was nine o'clock, the boys came in to select seats as far from the girls as possible. Soon all were ready to salute the flag.

Rachel was a good reader and speller. David and Robert watched her as she used the dictionary with skill. Last spring when I tried to help the boys with phonics, they didn't seem interested. Before the first week was over Robert asked, "Can I do what she does?"

"Of course. You can do anything she can."

Nothing more was said, but I knew the boys weren't going to let a girl get ahead of them. One day David smiled when he had the correct answer to a subtraction problem that Rachel missed. He learned she wasn't perfect in everything.

For a long while Bert and Albert refused to have anything to do with Ruth. One day Albert asked her how to pronounce a word. From then on she became so helpful the brothers became her friends.

George and Larry offered to help Carol in every way. Since they were in the second grade and she was only in the first the boys swung the rope for her to jump and taught her how to kick a ball.

Soon after school began I had a letter from Professor Wilson from Chadron that surprised and pleased me very much. He was going to attend the teacher's convention in Scottsbluff the first week in October. He wanted to know if it would be convenient for him to see our sod house on Saturday before he drove back.

He wrote, "I'd like to tell my students I've been in a liveable soddy."

It was arranged he would eat our noon meal with us. That way he could return home before evening.

Although my parents had entertained an attorney and his guests from Pennsylvania, a doctor and his family, teachers, and other important people, this was the first time a college professor had come.

It was a delightful four hours and Mother had cooked one of her best chicken dinners.

As our guest prepared to leave he said, "I've been doubly blessed today. Not only did I see first hand that Treva lives in a sod house, but her family are twentieth century pioneers.

"Thank you, Mrs. Adams, for a wonderful dinner, and, Mr. Adams, I hope I haven't delayed your harvest too much with my visit today."

As the two men shook hands, Dad said, "Our potatoes are in the cellar and there's no big hurry about husking the corn. It was our pleasure to have you here today."

The professor turned to the girls. "Dorothy and Helen, I hope I see you in one of my classes some day. I'm sorry your brother doesn't attend our college, but I'm sure he enjoys the university and all its activities."

Dorothy smiled, "After I graduate I plan to go to Chadron. I sure want to be in one of your classes."

Helen said, "So do I, some day."

Professor Wilson gave me a warm handshake before he entered his Dodge. "Stop in to see me the next time you're up to Chadron and thank you for making the arrangements for this memorable day."

I was so overcome with emotion I could just say, "Good-bye. I'll see you next summer."

One Saturday in October, I thumbed through the Montgomery Ward fall and winter catalogue looking for a dress for the holidays.

My eyes lighted upon an all wool bright red dress for eight dollars. Henry said he liked me in colors that seemed to express my personality, so I sent for it.

Two weeks later when my sisters returned home from school they had found a notice in the mailbox that a package had come for me. It had been left at the farm house near the mailbox where the girls got off the school bus. They decided since I had my car, they didn't need to lug it home.

"That's all right," I said. "Now I can test my Model T's ability to climb the hill when I return."

Dad frowned. "You better take the long way home. Our Dodge won't go up it, so there's no use to attempt it in your car."

"I'll never know unless I try."

"O.K. Go ahead, but I doubt you'll have any luck. I think the only way that would be possible would be for you to back up the hill. That gas tank under the seat just can't feed the engine when you drive up a steep hill."

"You mean the pull of gravity keeps the gas in the tank instead of in the engine?"

"Yes, so the only way you could use it, is to back up."

I shrugged. "No problem, you taught me a long time ago how to back up."

"Good luck. If any one is brave enough to try it, I guess it's you."

Dorothy agreed. "I'll ride with you to the mail box, but I'll walk up the hill while you try to get over it."

Helen said, "I'll go too. I don't want to miss out on anything. I won't ride up the hill either."

Before we left Mother cautioned, "Treva, do be careful."

The girls took turns opening and closing the two gates on the mile and a half trip to the mailbox.

I put the Ford in low as we went down the steep incline so I wouldn't lose control. I wondered if I could return that way, but I sure wasn't going to express my doubts to my sisters.

The package was deposited in the trunk and off we started home. The girls climbed out at the foot of the hill. I made a run for it. The motor sputtered and stopped. I used the foot brake to slow the descent. I tried once more with no luck. Then I turned the car around. Slowly, but surely, I backed up the incline and waited for the girls to reach the top.

As we traveled along Dorothy said, "That success story will be in my next letter to Norman. Bet he'll be surprised as I was."

I couldn't wait to reach home to brag on my car's achievement.

By the first of December the nine pupils were like one happy family, so I asked if they'd like to prepare a Christmas program for their parents. The girls were so enthusiastic the boys finally decided to agree. With cardboard and a few boards we fashioned a fireplace. It took two packages of crepe paper that resembled bricks to cover the structure. Each child brought a stocking to hang on it. We made wreaths of construction paper to decorate the windows. They memorized songs and poems. Each pupil designed and wrote an invitation to his parents. David and Rachel made copies of the program. Mrs. Lockwood volunteered to bring cookies.

On the day before vacation Mr. and Mrs. Armstrong and Mr. Jackson arrived at noon although the program would not begin before one. The boys spent the hour telling their parents about our activities and showed them the new books and other supplies.

When the girls' parents came, Rachel, who announced the program, asked Larry to give the four line welcome. When he stood before the group he just looked into space while his lips began to quiver. I smiled and whispered the first line. He mumbled that sentence and hurried to his seat.

The girls sang "Up On The House Top" in good voice and remembered all the motions. Ruth pretended she was skating and Carol rocked her doll. They did so well the boys relaxed and performed their parts in an acceptable manner. Although "Twenty Froggies" wasn't a Christmas song the boys sang it anyway. At the end of each verse they imitated the frog's croak. How everyone laughed!

While the adults enjoyed the refreshments they talked about their school days. By three o'clock all were ready to leave and start our vacation.

The week passed quickly with many activities and 1929 began with temperatures hovering between twenty and twenty-five degrees below zero at night with a high of fourteen during the day. Henry felt his Ford was better than mine to withstand the cold so he volunteered to take me to my shack and come after me on Friday evenings. He said, "By the time your flivver stands for five days you won't be able to get it started again until summer."

Attendance at school was sporadic. Often Robert and I were the only ones there. When we reached our destination my hands were so numb I had difficulty turning the door knob.

In half an hour the stove had glowing red sides, but the frost didn't melt from the nails in the wall until noon. We scraped the frost from the windows so we could look out and let more light enter. Our desks formed a circle around the stove.

The children spent their free time playing dominoes, checkers and tiddlywinks. We brought our own drinking water since it was too cold for the boys to make the extra trip a half mile away. No one went outside except to go to the outhouse or bring in coal.

Everyone was delighted when it was warm enough for all nine pupils to attend.

It was on one of those days that the unexpected happened. I was helping the fifth graders understand long division when there was an obnoxious smell. "Pee-yew! Pew-yew!" Then I heard Carol sob.

David asked, "Can we go outside?"

"Yes, grab your coats and scoot. I'll need water. Boys, please get some in a hurry."

Not one piece of Carol's clothes escaped the disaster. After I helped her undress she put on her coat.

"Why didn't you ask to go to the toilet?"

"You were busy," she sobbed.

"If this happens again, you go without asking."

I couldn't scold. I washed her clothes and hung them on nails. This was a task I never associated with teaching. For the first time the boys shied away from her and the sisters seemed to be very protective. She was fortunate the clothes dried before dismissal because their car didn't have a heater.

January passed and February became a little warmer. Valentine's Day was nearly as exciting as Christmas. Although valentines could be purchased for a penny each, the children wanted to make some.

Rachel suggested, "Let's draw names. Don't show anyone whose name you have. Buy an extra nice one for that person."

The boys said they'd have to ask their parents if they would go to the store for valentines. "Pa went to town just two weeks ago," David said. "He may not want to go again soon."

"Same here," Robert agreed.

The next morning the boys from both families said their fathers would get the special cards, so the children drew names. I brought a large cardboard box to hold the valentines. After I made a slit in the lid the children decorated it with red crepe paper and handmade hearts. Mrs. Armstrong sent word she would bring refreshments.

The day before the event, David reported, "Our pas are going to have a surprise for us."

After everyone arrived Mr. Jackson said, "Today, us men are going to show you how smart we are. First, we're going to spell for you, and then we'll solve some problems. Miss Adams, you say the words and we'll spell them."

"All right, I'll start with the words the fifth graders are spelling this week."

The three men did fine until I asked Mr. Armstrong to spell 'scared'. "I scared the coyotes away from the house."

"S-c-a-r-t."

"No, that's not correct. Mr. Jackson, can you spell 'scared'?"

"S-c-a-r-e-d."

"That's correct."

Mr. Armstrong frowned. "That's not right. Let me see it in the book." He stared at the word. "I couldn't believe I didn't know how to spell it. Now I know why." He laughed. "Let's do arithmetic."

The men agreed. Mr. Jackson said, "Give us the hardest addition and subtraction you can find. We can multiply and divide, too. Olie, you and Ed go first and I'll beat the best of you."

I'd never seen the children so excited. In loud whispers I heard, "Hurry, Pa." "You made a mistake, Pa." "Jumpin' cracker jacks, I can do that one." "Hurry, hurry!" Finally Mr. Lockwood was declared the champion. His daughters clapped so long he shook his head and color rushed to his cheeks.

"Let's open the box. I can't wait to see how many valentines I get," Rachel said.

The boys didn't say anything, but their looks indicated anxiety too.

"David, will you be the postman and Bert, will you be the mailman?"

It was an enjoyable time. Some of the cards opened to standing positions. Most were pretty and had sentimental verses; only a few were funny. Little Carol received the most and everyone seemed pleased.

Before the parents left, Mr. Lockwood said, "I don't remember when I've had so much fun."

Mr. Armstrong smiled. "I'd better say 'scared' instead of 'scart' from now on so I'll know how to spell it next time."

Everyone laughed.

"Guess I'd better study arithmetic with David. He might challenge me some evening."

Both ladies expressed their pleasure. Mrs. Lockwood added, "I'm very pleased with the progress the girls are making. Every evening they tell their father and me about their activities."

Mrs. Armstrong said, "Yes, aren't we lucky to have Miss Adams?"

Since there wasn't room enough in the Armstrong car for an extra person I walked home alone. When my shack came into view I noticed smoke coming from the chimney and saw Henry's Ford. I ran the rest of the way, stamped the snow from my overshoes and pushed the door open.

"Henry! How nice for you to be here and have a warm room for me."

I gave him a quick hug and was delighted he responded with a kiss on my forehead. I'd become accustomed to his lack of showing affections.

"Well, you didn't expect me to sit here freezing while I waited, did you?"

"Of course not." I took off my coat and walked to the table. "What are in your packages and what is this?" I picked up an envelope and took out a valentine showing a girl and boy holding hands. I read:

> I always save my pennies
> And now and then a dime,
> So I can buy a wedding ring,
> For some nice girl on time.

My face felt hot so I must have blushed. Did this written message convey what Henry seemed unable to express verbally?"

"That's a nice verse." What else was I supposed to say? Did he expect me to propose to him? At least I had a feeling he liked me. It was best to change the subject. "What do you have here?" I picked up a package.

"I brought two steaks for our supper."

"That sounds good."

He reached into a small sack and brought out two potatoes. "Give me a knife and I'll peel this. I spent so much time doing K.P. while in the army I can do it easy." In seconds he accomplished the task and had one continuous peeling.

"You better do the rest. I don't want to spoil you."

Soon we had a good meal. After the dishes were washed we played two games of dominoes before he left.

It was the last week in March when Rachel surprised us by saying, "This is our last day. We're moving to a ranch where we'll be close to the school. We like it here, but we have to move."

The boys seem stunned by the announcement. "We sure will miss you," Robert confessed.

David added, "I learned girls are better than I thought they'd be."

In a silent expression of their regret, the younger boys let the girls go first in all the games. It was a sad day.

After the girls moved, the boys seemed to lose interest in their studies. They returned to games they'd enjoyed the spring before, but their enthusiasm was gone. It was then I started to look forward to the end of the term.

LOOKING AHEAD

Late in April I met an older teacher friend. "Treva, she said, "It's time for you to change schools. It's better to stay only two years in the same district. You do your best teaching that way. It's also good for the pupils and their parents to have a change."

"You're probably right, but how do I find another school? When I began the school came to me."

"Go see Mrs. Southwell, Scotts Bluff County's Superintendent of Schools. She'll tell you where to apply. You've stayed long enough in the ranch country."

At nine o'clock on the first Saturday in May, I parked my car in front of the two-story brick courthouse. My heart pounded as I rushed up the steps of the largest building I'd ever been in. The bare wooden floor creaked as I hurried across the entryway to the broad stairs. On the second floor, I read the sign above the various doors until I saw Mrs. Southwell's office.

A gracious, motherly-looking lady stepped from behind her desk to shake my hand. She was the only occupant in the large room. "What can I do for you, young lady?"

I explained my mission.

With a warm smile she said, "I have just the place for you. Sunny Slope, three miles north of Mitchell, will need a teacher this fall. Since Miss Gilbert is getting married, she won't return. There's so much unemployment, it's the county's policy to employ only single girls."

"That's a good idea."

"Let me think," she paused. "I believe you'd better see the Hartzes first. Both of them are on the board. If they like you, you'll probably get the position. Good luck."

Forty minutes later I stopped my car to look at Sunny Slope school. The white frame building stood in the middle of an area bare except for weeds around the edge. There in the yard were two outhouses, a coalhouse, a set of swings, two basketball standards with hoops, and a flagpole near the public road. A real school. Would it be mine?

A half mile north, I found the Hartz farm. Mr. Hartz was in the farmyard near the water tank removing the bridles from a team of matching greys. He was a large man in faded blue bib-overalls. He removed an old straw hat and ran his fingers through a mop of thick grey hair. I introduced myself and explained the reason for my visit.

With jovial lilt in his voice he asked, "Do you think you can handle a bunch of boys? There's a few small ones, but most are nearly as big as you. The oldest is probably sixteen."

"Do you mean can I give them boxing lessons? Sure, I've been boxing with my brother for over seven years. But I really thought you needed a teacher who would help them in the classroom."

"We do, but learning takes place outside as well as inside the building. You look all right to me." He turned toward a petite lady walking our way. "What do you think, Mother?"

As she shook my hand she said, "You sound as though you can handle our school. While we're eating go see the treasurer, Mrs. Garlow. She has the contract. If you hurry you'll get here before Dad goes back to planting corn."

I felt the blood rush to my cheeks. Getting a new school was easier than I had anticipated. "Thank you very much, I'll hurry. If I get the job, will you tell me where I can board and room through the week? I'll go home on weekends."

"You can stay with us for a dollar a day. You'll share a bed with our youngest daughter."

"Wonderful." I wanted to hug that lady whose hair was combed straight back into a neat bun.

I hurried back to my car, drove from the yard and followed Mrs. Hartz's directions to the other farm. My hand shook as I pulled down on the gas lever. If Mrs. Garlow would be as agreeable, I could be home by early afternoon.

When I knocked on the screen door, I heard a sharp, "What do you want?"

This startled me. "I'm Treva Adams. Mrs. Southwell suggested I contact the board in this district for a teaching position. I've talked with the Hartzes and they agreed to hire me if you approve."

A lady about my size stepped out on the porch. Her eyes squinted as she placed her hands on her hips and stared at me without comment. I felt my legs tremble and my thoughts ran wild. She doesn't like my looks. She doesn't like what I said. She won't give me a contract.

Finally she spoke. "My only daughter will be an eighth grader. Are you sure you're capable of helping her pass those state tests?"

"Mrs. Garlow, I know all about those tests." I bit my lips while thinking about them. "I had to take them too so I know how difficult they are."

The mother seemed to relax. "She's a good student. Now I have a second question. Do you like boys? My youngest son will be in the sixth grade."

I grinned and repeated my answers to the Hartzes' questions concerning my ability to work with boys. I added, "I was center on the high school basketball team, and I know the rules for baseball and football. Mr. Hartz says the school has a number of large boys so we should have some pretty good teams."

She rubbed her forehead as though deep in thought. In a solemn voice she said, "I believe you can handle the school. You wait and I'll fill out your contract." She abruptly turned and went into the house.

I didn't know what to do so I walked back to my car. As I leaned on the fender, I wondered if her children would want special favors since their mother was on the board. Soon she reappeared carrying the contract and I walked to meet her.

"These are hard times and we expect you to earn your salary." She spoke in a firm voice. "Plan to come to school a few days early, so everything will be ready for the first morning. If the pupils see you mean business, they'll settle down." She repeated, "Remember, we expect you to earn your salary."

I swallowed the lump in my throat trying to control my voice. "I'll do my best."

She gave me a faint smile. "You look like you would do that. I wish you luck." She handed me the contract. "If it's any of my business, what are you doing this summer?"

"I'm going to college to earn twelve units toward the renewal of my certificate."

She shook my hand. "That's good. We'll see you in September."

As I drove away, I decided Mrs. Garlow was not as cold and unfriendly as I thought at first. After I left the driveway, I stopped the car long enough to read the contract. "Nine months of twenty days each at one hundred dollars per month. Holidays: Thanksgiving Day, New Years's Day, and a week at Christmas. "One hundred dollars! Wow, whoopee, I'm going to be rich."

I hurried to the Hartz farm. They came to the car to sign the contract and to wish me well. As I drove past the school the second time, I slowed down. "You'll never be the same, Mr. Schoolhouse, after I take over."

From then on, I was anxious to see the end of the term. My teacher friend was right. It gave me a lift to know I was going to a different school.

On the following Monday I asked the boys if they wanted an end-of-the-year picnic. They looked at each other and then at me.

Larry said, "What's the use? There's nothing to do. It won't be any fun."

The others agreed. The boys had never recovered their enthusiasm for extra curricular activities after the girls left.

During the last week, the boys and I talked of many experiences we'd shared. They laughed about the spanking I'd given them. David and George said the homemade flag was still in their bedroom.

Robert said, "That ball we used for the world sure hated to be a plain old plaything again. And I've learned to use the pronoun in the right place."

"All of you have learned so much. I want you to know I have too. Although I won't be your teacher next year, I'm sure we'll always be friends."

When I handed them their report cards the last day, I hugged each one and promised to write to them. I felt like crying and I think they did too. Those boys would always be close to my heart when I recalled my first teaching experience.

SUNNY SLOPE SCHOOL—
CHANGING TIMES

A few days before I left to attend college classes in June, 1929, Norman said, "Sis, I'll make the last three payments on your Tin Lizzy if you'll let me use it this summer."

"That's a deal. Then I'll have forty dollars to spend on clothes. I need a couple of dresses and a pair of white slippers. Guess you know Henry's going to take me to Chadron next Sunday and he's promised to come over for my birthday."

"Yes, he told me. It should be quite a celebration."

"Just remember that's still my car and you aren't given permission to change it in any way."

He laughed. "Oh, you mean like that 1920 Dodge sedan Dad got in exchange for an old cow. It had to be towed home."

"Yes, I remember with little help from Dad you got it to run. For a fourteen year old you were a pretty good mechanic."

"Perhaps. That old car had a lot of problems and the worst was a flat crankshaft. Dad drove to a junk yard where I took a better one off a 1916 Dodge. He growled, but helped a bit to replace the old one."

We walked over and sat in a porch swing where he continued, "I didn't want any extra on it so I took the body off, hitched up the team and dragged it to the far side of the chickenhouse so the girls could use it for their playhouse."

I nodded. "How well I remember that. Mother complained at first that she didn't want any junk that could be seen from the house. You finally convinced her the chickenhouse would hide it."

"On the chassis I made one long seat that all four of us kids could crowd onto. I used old boards and orange crates. The car didn't have a license, but that wasn't necessary in the country."

Mother called that dinner was ready. As we started to go in the house I said, "I remember sometimes you drove us to Sunday School if Mother or Dad couldn't go. And one time when friends had a party you tied two kerosene lanterns on the front. That was really a scary evening as they didn't give much light. You never drove it again at night."

I gave him a stern glance. "Just remember, no monkey-business with *my* car."

I was ready and waiting when Henry came to take me to Chadron. It took three hours to drive the one hundred and twenty miles. The two-lane road was in good condition, since there had been little snow and rain that spring. Two years before when Dad took me, the ruts were so deep we didn't get there until evening. He had to stay all night and go home the next day.

This time hot, dry air created mirages every few miles. When we approached the first one, I was sure we were coming to a pond.

"Henry, look at all that water ahead of us."

It gave me a strange feeling when we arrived at the scene and saw only a dry dusty road.

Another time I thought I saw a grove of trees on either side of a pond. That, also, turned out to be an illusion.

Before we reached our destination we discussed the mirages. Henry appeared surprised I'd never seen one before.

The Strattons, where I'd stayed two years before welcomed me. After my belongings were settled in my room, Henry and I ate dinner near the campus. After taking me back to the Strattons he left for home.

It was good to be back with this congenial couple, but I remembered the husband had been concerned about his job. They worried the truckers would take all the business away from the freight trains. Mrs. Stratton didn't shop at any store that had their merchandise trucked in.

That was the first time I'd heard of discord in the commercial world and it made me aware that if I were to become a better teacher I needed to broaden my knowledge in areas other than farming and ranching.

As we sat at supper that evening I asked, "Has anything interesting happened here since I've been gone?"

Mr. Stratton smiled as he buttered a slice of bread. "Yes, we've learned there's room for both the railroads and the truckers. Nellie trades in any store she wants to now."

His wife said, "You have to remember Claude came from a family of railroaders. Like him, his father and grandfather were engineers. We really felt our livelihood was threatened when the truckers started competing."

"I'm happy to hear that's settled. Maybe it's similar to the time when automobiles first became popular. Remember how livery stables lost business until they gradually changed to garages?"

I experienced another first when a group of us went on Saturday evening to an open-pavilion dance. Indians from the Pine Ridge Reservation sat on the ground watching us. No one spoke to them and I wondered if they understood English.

It came as a big surprise when an Indian student spoke at a general assembly. "You consider us citizens when you want us to fight your wars, but you treat us like outcasts the rest of the time. You try to keep us on reservations and tell us what we can and cannot do. Shame on you!"

That forthright accusation disturbed me. That was the first time I'd ever thought about the plight of the Indians. No history book had informed me how the Indians felt when the white man claimed the land. I hoped some day an Indian would write a textbook to tell their side of the story. From then on I tried to better understand their problems.

When I entered into a debate during a discussion in a contemporary literature class concerning the "Scopes Monkey Trial" I recalled Mr. Hartz' remark about learning outside as well as inside the classroom. I did hope all these experiences would help me.

John Scopes, a twenty-four-year old high school teacher had taught the biological theory of evolution to his students although Tennessee law prohibited teaching a belief contrary to the Bible. The trial in 1915 became world famous when Clarence Darrow defended Scopes, but lost the case to William Jennings Bryan. Scopes was fined one hundred dollars.

The debate developed because Fred, a member of the class said, "I agree with Scopes and we should be able to teach what we believe. I, too, think we are derived from monkeys. Some of us are just smarter monkeys than others."

Without hesitation I declared, "I can't believe you'd say such a thing!"

Some agreed with me, but others sided with Fred so the professor suggested a debate. I spent hours in research and so did the other two on my team studying Bryan's position.

Although it is often said there are two sides to every question I could never convince myself that Scopes had the right to challenge the story of creation, so it was a great satisfaction to me that my team won.

Henry came for my birthday the last weekend in June. I was happy to see him and introduce him to my friends. They in turn enjoyed his wit and the chocolates he brought.

On Saturday we took another couple with us to visit Wind Cave in South Dakota. It had been discovered when a cowboy felt a strong current of air coming up through a crevasse in the earth as he rode across the prairie after a stray cow.

Our tour group had twenty adults and two children, with every second person carrying a gasoline lantern. I shivered as we entered the cave and felt the rush of cool air. We saw the stalactites and stalagmites as we slowly walked the mile course underground. Often we stooped low to get from one chamber to the next. When we reached our destination, the guide turned off each lantern and we stood in complete darkness.

I moved my hand in front of my face. How I wished my high school science teacher Mr. Ziegler, were there! He had taught it would never be too dark to see our hands in front of our faces no matter where we were. I realized two things: he had not been in Wind Cave and that some teachers make mistakes.

Although I had to admit Mr. Ziegler was a good teacher he and I were often in conflict with our ideas.

One morning I walked into class and announced I knew I'd get an A in the test we'd take that day because my brain had slipped forward.

As I started to my seat, he cleared his throat. "Treva, most people's brains fill their head and don't slip around."

I turned and eyed him up and down. "If my brain moves around, I at least know I have one."

The class laughed, but that didn't bother me. When my test was returned the next day there was an A on it and a comment, "Those brains you know you have must work well."

The stillness gave me a spooky feeling and drove memories of Mr. Ziegler from my mind. I reached for Henry's hand. When a man's voice broke the silence with "Hey!" the sound echoed back from all directions. The children began to cry. Soon others called out a word or two until the cave became filled with shrill and muffled tones and echoes. What a relief I felt when the guide struck a match to relight the lanterns so we could go back to the opening.

The four of us returned to Chadron late that afternoon. My twentieth birthday had been a joyous time because Henry had come and my friends had shared the day.

From then on, I was eager for the twelve weeks of summer classes to end, but I knew my little world had begun to expand and I came to the decision that the pupils at Sunny Slope were going to be better informed about conditions and events than I had been.

Now it was time to look forward to the beginning of school. When Dad arrived in the middle of August, I was packed and ready to leave.

Early on the last Monday of the month I drove to the Hartz farm. Mrs. Hartz greeted me when I asked for the key to the schoolhouse. "It looks as though you're anxious to get busy."

"I am. I've many things to do before the week is over."

I took the key. "I'll see you next Monday evening. Good-bye 'til then."

I waved, ran to my car and drove from the yard. In a few minutes I parked near the front of the school, unlocked the door, and hurried through the cloakroom to survey my new domain. It smelled of fresh paint. The walls were a soft cream color and the six window frames a bright green.

I stood at the entrance of the big room and chuckled. The coal stove which glistened like new with a fresh coat of polish was near the door and not in the middle of the room as the one at Wind Springs had been. The thirty-six desks of various sizes were nailed onto six pairs of long runners, so they would be easier to push into the aisles when I swept.

My footsteps echoed as I walked toward the teacher's desk in the front of the room. My heart pounded when I wrote "Miss Adams" in the dust on its top. I smiled and thought about all the boys and girls who would call me that in another week. Next I glanced at Lincoln's and Washington's pictures above the blackboard as I started to the back of the room to examine the stacks of textbooks on wide shelves. Nearby a narrow bookcase held a set of reference books and a dozen dog-eared dictionaries. I felt like shouting for joy as I walked back to my desk and sat in the teacher's chair.

I pulled out the large middle drawer to find a copy of the school census. Nineteen girls and sixteen boys were listed, with pupils in every grade from the first through the eighth. The oldest was fifteen, only five years younger than I.

During the week I stayed at home and drove the sixteen miles twice each day. Before leaving on Friday I boldly wrote my name across the top of the blackboard and the axiom: "All that you do, do with your might, for things done by half are never done right."

Monday morning, the first day of school finally arrived. Everything had to be just right. I smoothed the skirt of my red and white gingham dress. My brown curly hair lay in waves as though I'd been to the beauty parlor for a marcel. I wore no make-up, but felt satisfied with my naturally rosy cheeks and reddish lips.

As the car sped along toward Sunny Slope a song in a 1914 book kept running through my mind.

> Forty little urchins coming through the door,
> pushing, crowding, making a tremendous roar.
> 'You must keep more quiet, can't you mind the rule!'
> Bless me this is pleasant, teaching public school.

There were four verses, but I remembered only the first one.

At seven o'clock I parked my Ford near the front door, picked up my lunch pail, and hurried to unlock the building.

With a spring in my step I entered the cloakroom where I laid my lunch pail on the shelf above the coat and cap hooks. I stood for a moment at the door of the classroom. It was beautiful. For a second my glance rested on the globe and I thought of the one we made from a ball and pages from an old geography book at the other school.

I picked up the flag that was stored in a cupboard with other supplies. On my way to the front of the building, I unfolded the banner. How proud I felt as I pulled it to the top of the flagpole. This was a real school!

Soon the children began to appear. After saying "Hello" they hurried to the playground. A small blond-headed lad with a broad smile was the first pupil to stop long enough to talk.

"Hello, I'm Sport Garlow. Mom said you'll probably call me Albert. She also said I was to help. I rode my pony so I beat Virginia here." He paused and looked around the room. "It sure looks nice. Do you want anything?"

I shook my head. "No, but thanks for offering. I've wondered all summer what you looked like. Your mother mentioned you when she signed my contract." I picked up the census and gave it a quick glance. "I notice you're only ten and in the sixth grade. You must be a good student. I hope you like school."

"I sure do." He left to join his friends.

When Virginia arrived it surprised me to see such a small eighth grader.

"I may be tiny, but I'm mighty," she said. "Anyway the little kids like me. Shall I start them playing 'Ring Around The Rosy?' That's the game they like best."

"Thank you. How nice of you to offer. This is a pleasant surprise. It will give me more time to do other things."

Mary came at eight-thirty. "You'll have six of us Sniders. I'm the oldest with five younger brothers. I sure do worry about those state tests I'll have to take next spring."

I scanned the sheet before me. "I notice you passed the four last spring with good grades. I'm sure you can do as well on the other ten."

"I hope so. Anyway I don't look forward to them."

Just before nine Katherine Lind and her four younger brothers and little sister arrived. I glanced at the clock on the south wall. "It's time for school. Let's go outside."

I picked up a small hand bell from my desk and walked outside and stood on the edge of the porch. The children stopped playing when they heard the bell and walked quietly to the front of the building.

"Good morning, if I haven't greeted you. I'm happy to be your teacher and I hope you'll like school this year." I looked into thirty-five expectant faces.

"When you go in, select a seat that fits you. You older children will find the assignments on the blackboard and your textbooks are on the shelf at the back of the room."

"Please form two straight lines with the boys on the right. Before we go in we'll salute the flag and sing the first stanza of 'America.' "

After the song the pupils marched into the classroom to find seats. In a short time the room was quiet. For the next fifteen minutes I showed the first and second graders what they were to do and answered their questions. I knew no class period could be longer than fifteen minutes and some subjects would be taught every other day.

After an hour the little ones became restless, so I excused them to go outside to play. Five minutes later first grader Bently came running in screaming, "Clifford fell in!"

Fell in what? I knew it wasn't the well and hoped it wasn't the outdoor toilet. I started for the door and so did all the pupils. There was no order as we rushed outdoors. The older boys ran ahead to an irrigation ditch on the north side of the playgrounds.

By the time I reached Clifford he had been able to get onto his feet and was trying to climb out. Luckily the ditch was only half full of water. I held him firmly by the hand and pulled him up to stand beside me. I frowned. "How did you happen to fall in? What were you doing over here?"

Clifford started to cry so Bently answered. "We was trying to get to the other side of the ditch."

For the first time I saw a plank hidden by high weeds, spanning the ditch. I looked down at the six-year-old boy. "It's too bad you got in trouble the first morning you came to school."

I glanced at the three older girls. "I'd better take him home before he catches cold." Although it worried me to leave the children I felt concern for a child's health. "Do you think you can take charge?"

They assured me they could and the other pupils promised to be good. As I drove from the schoolyard I asked, "Where do you live?"

"Down there." He pointed west.

"Tell me when we get near your house."

In about ten minutes I knocked at the front door of an attractive yellow house. When the mother opened it she looked first at her child and then at me.

"Mrs. Snider, I'm Miss Adams. Clifford fell in the ditch. He'll have to stay home today."

She frowned as she twisted the edge of her apron. "I German. No English."

"He's wet. Clifford, you tell her. I've got to get back."

Upon my return it was a relief to learn no problems arose while I was gone. At noon some children ate their lunches on the shady side of the building

65

while others stayed in their seats. The first and second graders were dismissed at three-thirty and the others left at four.

My house cleaning duties began when I went to the coalhouse to get a small pail full of sweeping compound that was stored there in a large barrel. I scattered this combination of sawdust and oil under the desks to keep down the dust. It was five-thirty before my duties were over and preparation for Tuesday was completed.

I drove to the Hartz home with anticipation as I looked forward to meeting the two daughters and especially the one with whom I would share a room.

When I arrived she came out to meet me. "Hello, I'm Dorothy, your room-mate. I promise to give you one-fourth of the bed. That's what I gave Patty last year when she stayed with us. Mom says I've gained a little this summer, but I don't think so."

She was wearing a pair of men's faded blue overalls and a white shirt. Her short, light brown hair was parted in the middle. Her bangs nearly reached her eyebrows. When I saw her pretty complexion and delightful smile it seemed a shame she was so heavy.

As Dorothy helped carry my clothes in she said, "I'm fourteen and in the tenth grade. Have you any good-looking brothers my age?"

"No, only one and he's at the university."

"What a shame. I'll show you where you'll put your things in our room." As she pulled out a drawer in a chest she said, "You can use this one and hang your dresses in the corner of the closet."

While I put my clothes away Dorothy lay on the bed and munched on stick candy and jelly beans. I had just finished when Marion, her attractive older sister, came to tell me supper was ready.

There was a large group in the dining room. I was introduced to the married son and his wife, to the married daughter and her husband, but no one said anything about the three young men. I felt a bit embarrassed so just nodded and smiled at them.

Mrs. Hartz sat down at one end of the table. Mr. Hartz at the other end started passing food. I became perplexed when I noticed no one talked, but they manipulated their hands in strange ways and kept smiling. I put food on my plate, but ate little. My head turned from side to side as though I were a puppet.

Finally Mrs. Hartz came to my rescue. "The family decided to initiate you. I'm the only one who hasn't learned sign language. Our son Bill, on Dad's left and his friends are deaf. Bill invited them here to meet you."

I put my hand over my mouth and looked at everyone around the table as they began to laugh.

"You were so funny," Marion said. Then she and the others mimicked the way I had looked from one to the other before I understood what was going on.

As they made mirth of my ignorance I thought this would make and excellent excuse to introduce the study of our five senses to the whole school and it could be an inspiration to the older pupils to use the encyclopedia to learn about Helen Keller. Since she and I shared the same birth date I had read about her with great interest.

"You sure know how to imitate me. This is my first experience watching folks communicate with their hands. Tell Bill's friends I'm happy they are here. It's a great way to get acquainted with all of you."

After supper Bill wound the victrola and put on a record. His friend Jerry bowed and offered his hand for me to dance.

I was surprised he kept perfect time to the two-step. When the record stopped I asked, "Since he's deaf, how does he know the beat?"

"He feels the vibrations," Dorothy answered. "He says you dance very well. He wants to know how and when you learned to dance."

"That's quite a story. A family two miles south of us dug a large cellar, fifty by one hundred feet, for a dance hall. It had a cement floor and was named 'The Spud Cellar.'" I guess it was given that name because usually potatoes were stored during the winter in cellars like that.

"Whole families came every Saturday evening during the winter months. Every man paid one dollar that was given to the three member orchestra, consisting of a piano, a violin, and a guitar. Bunk-like shelves were built along the walls, so that when the children became tired they would have a place to sleep.

"There were square dances, polkas, fox trots and waltzes. We children joined in the polkas because we didn't need partners. That's where I got started."

Dorothy asked, "When and where did you start to dance with partners?"

"There in the Spud Cellar when I was fourteen or fifteen.

"My parents wouldn't permit me to date until I was a senior in high school, so I depended on Norman to take me to the dances in town when he was home.

"He was always the gentleman. It was his policy that a boy had to ask him for permission to dance with me. Most of them were classmates, but Norman never wavered in his decision.

"One time when he was dancing I accepted a dance with a boy I knew well. For the next three weeks, Norman wouldn't take me to the dances. Then he started to have flat tires on the Dodge and he needed me to hold the flashlight while he changed them, so I was in his good graces again."

At ten o'clock Dorothy and I went to bed. I was sleepy, but spent most of the night clinging to the edge of the bed, trying to stay away from her hot body. I'd brought a basin of water into our room before retiring, so early the next morning I took a bath and dressed. It didn't take long to eat breakfast, pack my lunch with food Mrs. Hartz placed on the table, and begin the half mile walk to school.

I'd gone less than half way when a pickup stopped. The farmer and his wife offered me a ride. When we were near the school I cautioned the driver to slow down.

"Why?"

"Because I get out here."

He looked at me in surprise. "You do? The teacher isn't here yet."

"She will be just as soon as you stop."

He laughed. "I thought you were a high school student and we were taking you to your school in town."

The Sunny Slope School and Treva's 1923 Model T.

MANY COMPONENTS
OF LEARNING

September passed quickly because the pupils and I enjoyed working and playing together. As soon as possible after my duties were completed on the twentieth day of teaching, I picked up the warrant Mr. and Mrs. Hartz had signed and hurried to Mrs. Garlow, the treasurer, to exchange it for my check.

It was nearly suppertime when I arrived home. I greeted mother, "Look, my first one hundred dollars! Tomorrow I'll deposit it in the Irrigation State Bank."

"No, you won't. Jimmy's bank closed its doors yesterday afternoon," she said and wiped a tear away. "Thank goodness that's not our bank, but we know plenty who were caught."

I stood, dumfounded. Although other banks in the area had closed I always heard the Irrigation State was as strong as the Rock of Gibraltar. Jimmy Classelman, a bachelor, was known for his thrifty living and cautious investments.

An hour later, Henry arrived in an old car. "Where in the world did you get that thing?" I exclaimed.

He was so upset, he could hardly speak. "Yesterday I sold my Ford, put the money in Jimmy's bank at two, and an hour later it went broke." He started to stutter so he rubbed the side of his nose until he was calmer. Then he continued, "I was to buy a new Dodge this morning. This is the third bank that has closed in my face."

I felt like crying. I'd never known anyone who tried so hard to save money. "Oh, Henry. I'm sorry." I wanted to take him in my arms, but I knew this would embarrass him.

He threw his head back, "I'm not going to use a bank again. From now on I'm going to store my money in my sock."

It surprised me he could jest about this tragedy, but I blurted out, "That should make a strong bank." I held my nose.

Dad and Mother sat in their favorite rockers listening. Then Dad said, "I don't believe I could joke if that had happened to me."

Henry shrugged. "Well, I don't know what else to do. Maybe I can find a tree that grows dollars."

I took his hand. "I'm so proud of you. Now tell us where did you get that terrible looking car?"

"From a friend. He said I could use it until I can arrange to buy another one."

Dad cautioned, "From now on, we all better be careful where we invest our money."

The men discussed the two banks that were still open in town. After listening, I decided to deposit my check in the Scottsbluff National. If it had come two days later, I'd have been in the same predicament as Henry.

The following Monday, several pupils discussed their losses. William said, "From now on I'm going to spend my money as fast as I earn it."

"Same here," Albert agreed. "I had sixty-eight dollars toward a horse. I even had her picked out."

As the pupils continued to tell about their accounts in Jimmy's bank, I thought how I had earned money to buy school supplies and some of my clothes. When I was five, Dad promised Norman and me each a dime if we could pile more driftwood during the week than he could haul home in one trip on his make-shift sled. The wood had heated our tent home on the prairie.

I was nine when Dad gave me a penny for each one hundred potato bugs I picked from the plants, and a penny for each leaf that had hundreds of eggs on the underside. I put the bugs and leaves in a pail with a small amount of kerosene. When I returned from the field, I counted and recounted the bugs to be sure I hadn't cheated.

Between the ages of ten and fifteen, I trapped gophers, common enemies of the farmers. With their sharp claws they dug holes in the irrigation ditches. Sometimes the escaped water washed out the entire crop. The sheriff encouraged the destruction of these pests by paying twenty-five cents for each pair of front claws brought to his office.

During my junior and senior years I caught skunks. Since Norman was attending the university I used his traps. Dad taught me how to skin and stretch the hides.

The most gruesome job of earning money was skinning horses. Dad paid three dollars at farm sales for old ones that were barely able to walk to our ranch. He wanted them for hog feed.

If we'd skin the animals Dad offered Norman and me the hides that sold for five or six dollars each. Norman and I would split the money fifty-fifty.

My brother shot the horse in the head with his twenty-two and told me to start skinning on the neck. I couldn't begin until after the skin stopped qivering and I'd put a gunny sack over the eyes that stared up at me.

Since the skin on the neck was loose I couldn't skin as fast as Norman who worked on the firm part of the body. He bragged on how much he achieved and tried to convince Dad that I should only get one-third of the money. Dad didn't agree, so I received my half.

Before the day was over I learned how the pupils earned their money. All helped their parents and none were given an allowance without working.

That evening I paid Mrs. Hartz the twenty dollars I owed for September's board and room.

The next day after school was dismissed Albert returned to say, "Miss Adams, your papa's here."

When I saw Henry instead of Dad I was amused. He stood beside a new black Dodge coupe.

"Where did you get the money?" I asked in delight.

"I went to some of the men who owed me money. They had thought I was a bank when they were broke. Now I told them I was broke and wanted my money." He patted the hood of the car. "They gave me enough to buy this."

"It's beautiful, just beautiful! May I touch it?"

"Ya." He gave the hood another pat. "Always remember to clean your shoes before you get in. I'll help with your chores so we can take a ride."

"Wonderful. Let's hurry." I looked at him. "You do surprise me how you manage your money."

"So?" he said as we entered the school to begin the task. "It is better I loaned the money than to have it in Jimmy's bank."

As we worked I thought that if we married I would never have to worry about money. I felt Henry would always manage.

After we were in the car he said, "Look at this article in the paper. Jimmy Casselman claims he closed his bank of his own free will to save us depositors. He turned all his property over to the bank except his home. He claims the value of his property will cover the losses, so depositors will be paid in full."

I interrupted. "Does he say when you'll get your money?"

"No, but I hope soon. I need to build some fences on my farm."

"What else does he write.?"

"He tries to convince his depositors that he is honest. He says too often bankers think only of making a lot of money for themselves rather than for the depositors. That leads to unsafe, get-rich-quick banking."

I reached for Henry's hand. "I hope you and all others get your money back."

It was a good ride and I was happy that Henry could purchase a new car.

71

Most of the older students didn't attend school regularly during the last of September and the first of October. Their parents needed them to help harvest potatoes and sugar beets.

When the boys returned, they decided playing football was the most important part of their education.

"You boys can divide into two teams for practice. I have the rule book and I know most of the simple rules. When you're good enough we'll challenge another school."

"You mean you'll coach us?" Harry asked.

"Yes. But keep in mind, when we're outdoors, that's playtime, and when we're inside that's worktime. If you waste it and are kept in, that means no football practice for you and no coaching for the rest of the team."

The boys looked at each other and shrugged as though they understood I meant what I said. They disciplined themselves so well they wasted little school time.

Ted had a cousin who played football in high school. One day he told the coach about our team and at eight o'clock the next morning Mr. Evans appeared. It didn't take him long to give a few instructions to the five boys who were already practicing. Before the coach left he promised to come as often as he could.

Soon the boys asked if I'd arrange for them to play Cottonwood, a two-teacher school located three miles west of ours. Mr. Garlow gave permission for his hired man to take the boys in his truck. When the big day came I sent the first, second and third graders home at two. Seven girls crowded into my car with me.

A high school senior refereed the game. Cottonwood had a large cheering section. The Sunny Slope girls were few, but demonstrated great enthusiasm as they yelled and sang.

The boys on both teams were about the same size and age. After fifteen minutes of play, we'd made three touchdowns and they hadn't scored. The referee blew the whistle for the rest period. The Cottonwood team sat on the ditchbank and cried. All refused to finish the game. For days afterwards the children discussed the poor sportsmanship they witnessed at Cottonwood School. I felt proud of their regard for fairness.

Soon it was too cold for football so the pupils spent their free time playing dominoes and checkers.

It was on one of these cold mornings in November that I came into the Hartz kitchen to see a small boy leaning on crutches.

"Miss Adams, this is Billy. He'd like to ride to school with you," Mrs Hartz said.

"Hello, Billy. Where do you live?"

72

"Across the road at Uncle Abe's."

I had been several times at the Hartz's daughter and son-in-law's home. Billy was a surprise to me.

"Erma thought you would save her a trip if he could ride to school with you," Mrs. Hartz explained. "He just came last evening after living with other relatives."

As we were ready to leave the door opened and Mr. Hartz came in from the farmyard blowing his hands to warm them. "Where's your mittens, Billy?"

"At home. I mean at Uncle Abe's."

Mr. Hartz laughed. "That's a good way to keep from wearing them out. Just hope your fingers don't freeze."

I helped Billy climb into the car and we were on our way. At school the older boys often carried him on their shoulders. They had to be careful with the braces on both legs.

"Will he always have to wear them?" Clifford asked.

"Yes, I think so. Two years ago he had polio."

Billy tried to be independent and often did things that worried me. Abe said, "Don't baby him. His life hasn't been easy in the past and it won't be in the future. I'd like for you to help him be as self-reliant as possible."

It was about a week later that Billy gave the civics class a good excuse to have a court session. He was waiting for a ride home and Clifford and Austin were waiting for their older brothers. Clifford ran in to say Austin and Billy were fighting. I told the pupils to stay in their seats when I hurried outdoors.

Billy leaned on his crutches trying to strike back at Austin. When they saw me the boys stopped fighting. "You'd better come in and sit until school is dismissed."

As soon as we entered the classroom Harry asked, "Can we have a trial?"

"Since you've been studying the county, state and federal courts this should help you to better understand the system."

The two small boys sat on chairs near my desk while a jury was selected and Mary was appointed as judge. Then Billy and Austin each chose a friend who would serve as his lawyer.

"Why did you fight?" the judge asked.

Austin said, "'Cause we agreed to."

Billy added, "He said he could lick me and I told him he couldn't."

The lawyers proposed that if each boy said he was sorry the jury could decide what the punishment would be. Austin stood looking at the floor with his lips protruding, both hands clenched tight to his sides.

Using his crutches for support, Billy reached out and pulled his classmate's left hand upward as he said with dignity, "Austin, I'm sorry I hit you." Billy

73

pumped the hand up and down a few times. When he released it Austin's hand went close against his body again.

As I watched I decided Billy would make his way through life in an admirable manner and wondered what kind of man Austin would become.

The jury asked the judge if they could vote. Permission was granted.

"Your honor," the foreman began after a short consultation with the group, "Since Billy said he was sorry he can go home."

Austin said, "Then I'll say the same thing."

Billy extended his hand, Austin shook it once and said, "Billy, I guess I'm sorry I hit you."

The jury voted to excuse Austin. The judge looked at the clock on the wall and said, "Miss Adams, it's five minutes after four. Don't you think we'd better dismiss the whole court?"

"Yes, and I'm very proud of the way you all conducted the trial."

Soon Thanksgiving had come and gone, which meant in less than four weeks it would be the Christmas holiday. I didn't know who was the most excited, the pupils or I. All of them volunteered to be in a program we planned to give the Friday evening before vacation.

We decorated the room with wreaths made from construction paper, and red and green crepe paper chains. The Garlow family went to the hills south of the North Platte River to cut a pine tree. It made the classroom smell Christmasy.

The next morning children from three families brought strings of popcorn, and two others proudly held up cranberries they had strung on heavy thread.

"I popped enough corn to fill a wagon box," Mary said. "My brothers just stood around eating it until Mamma reminded them they were as responsible for the looks of the tree as I." She snickered and continued, "Mamma sure can straighten those five brothers out when she needs to. She's learning to speak more English, but when she really wants to lay down the law she talks in German."

Virginia held up her string of cranberries. "Papa complained it was a waste of money to buy these to put on the tree, but I told him we had to do our share to make it pretty."

The week before the program we took the lamps from their brackets above the windows, washed and shined their chimneys, and refilled them with kerosene.

At one time Sunny Slope had been a two-teacher school. The only evidence that remained was a wooden partition in the middle of the classroom that hung down two feet from the ceiling. Since we needed a stage, we stretched a wire from this partition to the north wall about four feet from the front of the room.

The Sniders, the Linds, the Garlows, and Benny Webber's grandmother donated the use of white bed sheets for the stage curtains.

The afternoon before the program the children asked, "When shall we come back, Miss Adams?"

"The entertainment begins at seven-thirty so try to be here at least ten minutes before. I'll come early to light the lamps."

By seven the adults had squeezed into all the seats while the little children sat on top of the desks. The older brothers and sisters arranged themselves along the wall at the back and sides of the classroom. The pupils sat crosslegged on the floor. There were buzzing sounds as guests quietly visited with their neighbors until Benny Snider stood before the audience.

> We thank you all for coming,
> And hope you'll come again,
> We wish for you the Christmas wish,
> For peace, good will to men.

He bowed and ran to his place on the floor while the audience clapped. Then came plays, songs, pantomimes, and other short readings. After each, the audience applauded loud and long. The pupils smiled to indicate they were happy the program was a success.

When Santa appeared the little children clung tightly to their mothers. A few cried. Then they timidly accepted the candy and nuts in homemade red cheesecloth stockings. The older children whispered. "That's Raymond Hartz. He's so skinny he needs more pillows."

As the happy group said their good-byes I felt it was a wonderful way to celebrate the holiday.

I went home for a week's vacation. Henry came nearly every evening for supper. Afterwards he joined the family as we played dominoes and checkers.

When he came on Christmas Day he brought books for Dorothy and Helen, a box of shotgun shells for Norman, a pipe for Dad, and a purse for Mother.

I watched everyone open their presents and wondered if I would get one. Finally Henry brought a small box wrapped in red foil from his pocket.

"This is for you." He held up a card. "It says so right here."

My fingers turned to thumbs as I tried to untie the white ribbon around the gift.

Helen came to stand beside me. "Do you want me to help?" she offered. "Hurry up, I want to know what it is."

"I do too." I looked at her and smiled. "But I want to save the ribbon and paper so I'm being careful. Just give me time."

Before I finished unwrapping the present Dorothy leaned over the back of my chair. Soon I held up a string of smooth pink beads with five sparkling rhinestones in the middle of the strand.

"Oh, Henry, they're beautiful!" I jumped from my chair to hug and kiss him on his forehead.

After I sat down again he reached over and patted my hand as though he felt embarrassed to show affection in the presence of the family.

Helen stuck out her tongue. "Ugh, this is too much for me. I want to get out of here."

"So do I," Dorothy said. "I need fresh air after all this."

Norman asked, "Dorothy, are you going with me to get a coyote? You know I always kill one every Christmas. Its skin means ten dollars for a new pair of boots."

"No, not today. Helen and I are anxious to try our new clamp-on skates."

Norman looked a bit unhappy as he opened the door to leave. "Then guess I'll have to get one by myself. Don't fall down too many times."

When the girls slung their skates over their shoulders to leave, Mother cautioned, "Don't lose your skate keys." Then she went to the kitchen to begin preparations for dinner and Dad said he had a few more chores to finish.

After they left I explained to Henry, "This is the first year since Dorothy got her twenty-two that she hasn't gone with Norman."

Henry appeared surprised. "Dorothy has a rifle?"

"Yes, when she was ten that was the only thing she wanted for Christmas. She couldn't show any enthusiasm for a new book by Zane Grey or the Ouija Board.

"After we looked at all the gifts, Norman asked Dorothy to give him his rifle from the stack of guns in the corner of the dining room.

"Right in front was her gun. Talk about joy. She hugged that gift like it was a doll. I don't think she shot it that first day, but it was probably the best gift she's ever received until she found her skates this morning."

"Found?" Henry asked.

"Yes, Dad wrote a note and put it in Mother's stocking. It said she'd find her gift outdoors. We kids went out to help her.

"On one branch of a cottonwood tree Mother found a necklace and on a branch in another tree Dorothy found her skates."

"Have you always played tricks on each other like this?"

"Oh, yes, I remember before we children had money to spend on presents, we wrapped pieces of coal in newspapers, put them in empty shoe boxes and put Dad's name on them. Of course we wrote a note and signed it 'Santa.' "

Henry grinned. "I saw Helen had a pair of skates also. Were hers hanging in a tree too?"

"Oh, Henry, you know Dad would never pull a trick on her. She's his pet. Her skates were on the chair where she hung her stocking."

"Did you hang one too?"

"Sure, we all do. That keeps Christmas alive. I got a pair of gloves. It's too bad you weren't here early enough to put your gifts on the chairs."

With a twinkle in his eyes he said, "Next year." He picked up the beads he'd given me and fastened them around my neck.

"I can't believe you'd give me such a lovely gift."

"That's all right. That's all you'll get until your birthday. If I marry you, I don't want you spoiled."

The Sunny Slope School football team.

The second-term class at Sunny Slope School.

NEW PUPILS

There were few days during January and February that the temperature rose above freezing by noon. Although I had a fire started by seven-thirty the room was so cold the children huddled around the stove until classes began. The ones who sat farthest from the heat wore their coats until mid-morning.

Since thirty-five pupils cannot be confined all day, every noon we went outdoors for at least fifteen minutes to run races or play "Fox and Geese" if enough snow covered the ground. One of the oldest boys went out a few minutes early to tramp a large circle in the snow then crisscrossed the area to make eight paths. The "safe base" for the geese was the center of the circle. Whenever they left it the fox would try to catch them. Whoever was caught became the fox.

In March a few farms were sold or had new renters so some children left and others arrived to take their places.

It was early that month when identical twins, Donald and Douglas, moved into the district. None of us could tell the brown-eyed sixth graders apart. Even the freckles that covered their noses and cheek bones seemed to be in the same places. The boys were very patient about identifying themselves and never tried to trick us as we continued to look for clues.

One morning Albert came to my desk. As he put his arm around my neck he whispered, "I know something. One has the bib of his overalls inside his vest, and the other has his bib on the outside. Now if we know which did which, we'll know who's who."

"Why don't you ask them?" I had to admire Albert's effort to solve a puzzle that bothered all of us.

He asked. They answered. So for one day we were able to tell them apart, but usually as one first grader said, "They look the same every day."

School ran smoothly until the Barrett family moved into the district. Mr.

Barrett had been hired as a ditch rider so the family lived in a company-owned house near the ditch. His job was to turn the water on and off for irrigating the farms in the area. He also kept a record of the amount of water each farmer used, since the water was rationed according to the number of acres under irrigation on each farm.

Clyde Barrett, a seventh grader, had his sixteenth birthday in February. His red hair was plastered down with what the boys called "axle grease." His filthy clothes could almost stand by themselves and when he walked past the other pupils they held their noses.

"Look at the scabs on his arms," Alec whispered. "He stinks. I get sick to my stomach when he gets near me."

I wanted to hold my nose too, but I had to figure how to help Clyde before I criticized. My family had little income when I was his age, but we were clean. Mother washed our clothes in the washing machine with homemade soap and water heated on the cookstove. We children took turns at pushing a handle back and forth for ten minutes to agitate the dasher in the machine which helped to clean the garments. If they still had spots Mother lathered them with soap and scrubbed the soiled places on the washboard.

Clyde's sister Alma, fourteen, was also in the seventh grade. As I looked at her dirty, stringy, blond hair, I thought how attractive she could be if only she would smile and have clean, well-fitting clothes. She seldom volunteered any information, but seemed able to answer when questioned.

Freckled, blue-eyed Betty appeared so uninterested in everything I wondered if she were healthy. She looked underweight and dragged her feet when she walked. Betty gave the fourth grade boys no competition in any learning situation.

Mark, the youngest, resembled Clyde, but was more sociable. He excelled in sports and the younger children admired his ability. He was nine and in the third grade.

As the days grew warmer the offensive odors became stronger. Since the children had come from the city schools, I decided to visit the superintendent for suggestions and advice.

Mr. Anderson shook his head. "If you can clean that family up you'll earn every cent of your pay. When the children were in our school, we sent the nurse to the home. It didn't do any good."

He reached for a small book on a shelf beside his desk. "I believe you are familiar with the Nebraska law as it relates to attendance."

Mr. Anderson thumbed through the book until he came to a page that looked as though it had been fingered and read many times. As he laid his hand on the page to keep the book open he quoted it almost verbatim. "Unless

80

children are excused due to illness they can be absent no more than twenty days during the one hundred-eighty day term."

"Yes, I know that, and according to their report cards they've been absent more than that."

The superintendent looked serious and nodded in agreement. "Yes, unfortunately. For this reason we couldn't kick them out because they smelled so terrible, but only waited and hoped they'd take a bath and wash their clothes." He paused. "Naturally we breathed a sigh of relief when they moved from the district."

"And Sunny Slope was the lucky school to get them."

Mr. Anderson stood. "I'm glad you can joke about it. All I can say is good luck. I have a feeling you'll handle the situation."

After my conference, I decided if there were to be any changes it would be up to me, so I visited the home.

Clyde met me at the door with a look of defiance when I told him I had come to see his mother. Without smiling he pushed open the screendoor where I saw a thin, distraught looking woman who wore a soiled cotton dress, sloppy shoes with over-run heels and a mop of uncombed hair pulled back in a knot.

"Mrs. Barrett, I came to ask if you could send the children to school cleaner."

"We ain't got no soap or a well. My man brings water for me so I kin cook. Do you want to sit down?"

"Thank you." As I walked across the room to a straight-backed chair near a table covered with dirty dishes something stuck to the sole of my shoe. I glanced over to notice the four children who sat on a couch covered with a faded green cloth. "You have a cookstove and you surely have buckets so Clyde could carry water from the irrigation ditch just outside your house." I reached into a paper bag. "I brought two bars of laundry soap and here's a cake of Ivory for baths." I laid them on the table. "When I was a child my mother took our clothes more than a quarter of a mile to the lake to wash them. We melted snow in winter to take baths. We were poor, but we were never dirty."

Mrs. Barrett sat down near me and stared at the soap. "I kain't pay you for these."

What a weakling this woman was in comparison to my mother!

"I don't expect you to. Your children have been absent more than the Nebraska law allows so they must attend school every day from now on." As she continued to look down I felt sorry for her, but I continued. "Your husband could be put in jail for breaking this law." I paused then hurried on. "I must also tell you that parents are threatening to send the sheriff to your home if the children don't come to school cleaner."

She looked with sad eyes from the soap to the children. I felt emotional,

81

but I dared not show it. "Mrs. Barrett, I hope you understand that I'm trying to help. Alma really wants to learn so she can finish her schooling and get a job."

As she picked up the bars she promised, "I'll see what I kin do."

I didn't dare show my elation, but as I rose to go my knees shook. I extended my hand to her. "Thank you. I really don't want you and your husband to get into trouble with the law and I want your children to be accepted by the other pupils. I'm sure if they're clean it will help."

I turned to the four children. "I'll see you in the morning."

Tears trickled down Mrs. Barrett's cheeks as I left the room. I hurried to my car, turned to wave at the family and drove to the Hartz farm hoping my visit would bring results.

For the next week the children did wear cleaner clothes and they did smell better, but soon it was nearly the same as before. Alma was the only one who continued to keep clean. I knew Clyde wouldn't be in school the next term, and maybe Betty and Mark would change for the better.

A few days later I was watching the older boys practice baseball while the younger ones played marbles. It was a school rule that after all the marbles had been knocked from the ring they were to be returned to their owners.

When I heard a childish voice call my name I turned to see Clifford running toward me. Tears streamed down his cheeks. "Mark won't give back my marbles. He gives them to Clyde."

I followed Clifford across the playground where Clyde and the younger boys waited. I extended my right hand. In a quiet, but determined voice I said, "Clyde, please give those marbles to me."

"No."

I repeated, "Clyde, will you please give me those marbles?"

"No, they ain't mine. They're Mark's."

I wanted to shake him. "Oh, no they aren't. They belong to Clifford. It's against school rules to play keeps. I didn't make the rule. I'm just supposed to see it's followed."

His face looked sullen. "They're Marks's and I'm just holdin' them for him."

I walked toward Clyde. He backed to the very edge of the playground. I was determined he would give me those marbles so I never gave a thought to what would happen if he refused.

"I'm asking you for the last time to give me those marbles." Again I extended my hand. "I've been the best friend you've had since you came to Sunny Slope. When the boys gang up on you, I help you. I gave you two of my brother's shirts and I've given you extra help so you can pass the state tests."

He spat on the ground, kicked the dirt, and pushed his hands deeper into his overall pockets. He glared at me. "I don't care if I don't pass those tests. I'm already sixteen so I'll never have to go to school again." He spat again. "I'm only going now because my dad says I have to. I hate school. I hate you. I hate all these kids." He turned back to face me. "All right, take these old marbles! They're cheap ones anyway. There's not a 'aggie' or a 'steely' in the bunch."

He didn't hand them to me, but threw them with such force they scattered in every direction. Clifford and his friends scurried to pick them up. They found all but two.

"It's past time to go in." I motioned toward the schoolhouse. The children quietly followed me into the building. I wanted to sit at my desk and weep in relief, but I conducted the classes as though nothing unusual had happened.

Late that afternoon while I swept, I thought what could have occurred if Clyde hadn't given up the marbles. He was four years younger than I, but taller and heavier. If he'd gone off the playground I would have had no jurisdiction over him although I'm sure he didn't know this. I recalled how the older pupils watched the dispute with grim and determined expressions on their faces. I felt sure they needed only a signal from me and they would have subdued Clyde if he had not handed over the marbles. I shuddered and hoped for better days.

When Alma came the next morning she said her brother had gone to work with his father. Since Clyde was sixteen and not interested in learning I was relieved. Better days had come quicker than I thought.

The twins at Sunny Slope School.

THOSE NOTORIOUS TESTS

It was no wonder rural eighth graders dreaded the state tests they had to pass in order to attend high school. I had them myself at Lake Alice School and remembered what a wide range of subject matter they covered.

In March when Mary, Virginia and Katherine began to prepare for them, the girls brought copies of the four they had taken and passed the previous May.

Mary said, "Before I took the one on Agriculture I practiced naming the breeds of all the animals and fowls on the farm." She laughed. "Dad was so proud he had me entertain his friends. Some opened their mouths in surprise when a girl could point out differences in the various breeds."

As she talked I recalled how difficult it had been for me to prepare for that test since we had only Leghorn chickens and our cattle were of mixed breeds. Our horses were just horses as far as I was concerned.

"What did you think of that test, Katherine?"

She cupped her chin in her hands. "I didn't like it either, but the one on bookkeeping was easy. If I didn't have to help Mother with the little brothers I'm sure I could get a job in a business office."

I glanced at the test. "It sure covered everything, from writing checks and receipts to balancing the ledger. Virginia what are you thinking about?"

She giggled, "Since I like only happy thoughts I try to remember the ones on penmanship and art, and forget the others."

Now it was time to concentrate on the ten they had to take in April.

Besides being accurate in computing square root, finding the circumference of a circle, and being able to work all forms of simple arithmetic, the pupils must be prepared to solve "thought" problems.

Katherine sighed, "I know how to figure the number of rolls to paper a room of a given size, and I can find the tons in a haystack if I know its height

85

and circumference, but the craziest thing is how to find the cords in a pile of wood. Don't you agree, Miss Adams?"

"I sure do. Since trees are so sparse in Western Nebraska, none of us would recognize a cord if we saw one. The dictionary states it's a stack of wood 4×4×8 feet. I guess that's large enough we wouldn't stumble over it."

Since there were thirty-two other children who needed my help the eighth graders had to study by themselves. The three huddled in a corner of the room to memorize the names and locations of all the bones in the body, trace the circulation of the blood and practice drawing a diagram of the eye in preparation for the physiology exam.

The children pulled down maps from a box on the wall for the location of the world's largest rivers and highest mountains. Texts and the encyclopedia were used for information about the principal cities and their industries.

Once each week I took the time to query the three girls concerning events that affected our country and asked them to give the dates. They also learned when the thirteen colonies were settled and by whom.

I hoped they could memorize the duties of the judges in the county and state courts and know the names of the judges in the Supreme Court long enough to pass the Civics test.

The grammar test always required diagramming simple, compound and complex sentences. This meant knowing the parts of speech of every word in a sentence.

Reading, Spelling, English Composition and Mental Arithmetic completed the list. In this last one the teacher read problems that pupils solved mentally, writing only the answers.

Sixty per cent was a passing grade. If a pupil failed any exam in April he could retake it in May.

The day before the event, Mary said, "Miss Adams, I sure wish you could go with us to the high school. We won't know the teacher and probably none of the other kids who are there."

Virginia complained, "If we attended a town school we wouldn't have to take them."

"That's right."

"If city kids don't have to take them, why do we?"

Although I had explained this before the girls apparently wanted to have it repeated.

"Many rural children are needed to help on farms and ranches. The Nebraska law mandates a pupil must pass the tests or be sixteen before he can leave school. That means some smart kids can stay home when they're twelve or thirteen if their parents agree."

The following Monday the girls brought their test copies. "Boy, were they ever hard!" Katherine greeted me. "Look at this. Where's the Greater Antilles and what's an archipelago?"

I laughed to cover my embarrassment. "Are they some part of our bodies we forgot to study?"

"No, I don't think so. They were in the geography test."

We were relieved when two weeks later we learned all three had passed.

April meant more than tests to the boys in the third through sixth grades. It meant baseball!

Schools used the standard hard ball and had nine players on each team. The three bases and home plate were gunny sacks filled with sand. The distances between them were the same as for a professional ball field.

Cottonwood School challenged us with, "You beat us in football, but we'll wipe you off the map in baseball."

We accepted that challenge the following Friday afternoon. Again, Jake, Garlow's hired man, took the team to Cottonwood in the truck while the girls rode with me. Immediately upon arrival I noticed some of the host team looked larger than they did the previous fall. But then I reasoned, the district probably had acquired new pupils during the term the same as Sunny Slope.

To our delight we were winning. It was the seventh inning when a large boy became pitcher. I thought about questioning his age because he looked very mature. Instead I walked over to the batter and whispered, "Take it easy, Donald. He can't put you out." Then I stepped about six feet to the left of home plate.

Instead of throwing the ball to the batter, the pitcher turned and threw it at me. He hit my left arm just above the elbow. I grabbed my arm with my right hand, wondering if it were broken. I had never suffered such a sharp pain. Tears ran down my cheeks.

This was no accident. That boy did what he considered revenge because his school was losing. I was the scapegoat. As I started toward him my anger increased with every step. When I stood in front of him, I demanded, "Why did you do that? Who are you? How old are you?" My questions came with the speed of a bullet and my voice rose to a high pitch.

I looked into the face of a frightened teenager who stood like a statue. He didn't say a word and his hands hung limp at his sides. Did he realize the seriousness of his actions?

The upper grade teacher stepped beside him. Apologetically she said, "Miss Adams, this is Tim. He doesn't attend school anymore. I didn't know he was going to pitch. Honest, I didn't."

I blinked back tears of rage and pain. "But you didn't stop him. You are

87

as guilty as he." Through clenched teeth I stated, "As long as I'm the teacher at Sunny Slope, we'll never play this school again."

When I turned around the pupils rushed to me. Alec asked, "Are you hurt?"

"Shall we beat up on them, Miss Adams?" William wanted to know.

"Of course not." He didn't know how badly I wanted to knock every one of them down, especially that teacher. "We won't dirty our hands on them."

Mary exclaimed in horror, "Look at her sleeve. It's blown up! Your arm must be swelling. Alex, give me your pocket knife so I can slit her sleeve."

When that task was completed Douglas declared, "Your arm looks like a blue watermelon."

It felt numb, but I decided I could drive. "Let's get out of here, Jake, before there's more trouble. Load the boys."

The Cottonwood teacher and pupils stood at a distance in silence when we left. Perhaps most of them, like the Sunny Slope children, didn't want the game to end this way.

I didn't stop until we reached the Hartz home. The girls gave me hugs before they left for their homes and hoped I'd be all right by Monday.

Mrs. Hartz helped by Marion and Dorothy applied ice from the ice box. She said, "It's terrible for a school activity to end like this. I hope that boy's parents are told what he did."

"I was so mad, I nearly forgot I was a teacher. I wanted to lay him out."

Marion laughed, "Ha, that would have been a show and a half. I bet you could have done it."

The pain subsided, but the swelling hadn't by the time Dad Hartz came in from the field. He stood in the open doorway with mischief in his eyes. "So you decided to grow bigger muscles. That's a quick way to do it."

"Dad, this is no time to be funny." Marion scolded.

"That's all right," I said. "He wouldn't be who he is without his sense of humor. Maybe it'll help my arm get better." I smiled at him.

The girls applied ice packs until far into the night. By Saturday morning most of the swelling was gone, but my arm felt as though it were filled with lead, and it looked as though it had been painted the colors of the rainbow.

While we were eating breakfast I said, "I'd better get on my way. My parents will wonder what happened. We have an understanding that if I don't come home on Friday evening, I'll be there early on Saturday." I looked at Dorothy and Marion. "You both should have medals of honor for losing sleep. I don't know what I'd have done without you. Maybe I can talk Henry out of an extra box of candy for you. Perhaps he's been lucky at the punch board this week."

Marion shook her head. "It's too bad your folks don't have a telephone. Then you could just stay here this weekend."

"I know. We're two miles from the telephone line. It would cost a fortune for an extension." I stood. "I really have to go."

As Dorothy carried my suitcase to the car she said, "Don't forget to brag on me to your family. Tell them I'm a first class nurse."

"Will do." Then I started the motor and drove from the yard.

When I reached home Mother took a quick look. "You'd better see a doctor."

"No, it's much better than it was last evening. I have no broken bones." I looked in the mirror. "I guess it looks bad, but I'm sure it'll be all right soon."

That evening Henry looked at the swollen arm in disbelief. "I didn't know teaching was such a dangerous job. Maybe I should rescue you."

His concern surprised me. "Some day that might be possible." I liked Henry, but not enough to give up teaching.

"You take a chance. I may change my mind about you. It isn't every day you find someone like me."

I smiled as I shook my head. "That's for sure. And it isn't every day that you find such a good cook as my mother." I didn't want him to think he had the world by the tail. "You can come for dinner tomorrow if you bring a couple of boxes of candy for the Hartz girls. They sat up most of the night with me."

After playing a game of dominoes, Henry announced, "I've only one box so I'd better try to get another one." Then he turned to Mother. "Mrs. Adams, I hope you will welcome me tomorrow."

"Of course, Henry. I know you like cream pie so I'll make one."

"That sounds good. I'll be here at noon."

I walked with him to the car. He put his arm around me and the mischievous sparkle in his eyes turned to solemn concern as he bent to give me one of his rare kisses. "I hope your arm is better soon. Maybe I won't change my mind about you."

I returned his kiss and ran to the house with my heart fluttering. This was the warmest show of affection he'd ever revealed.

On the following Monday most of the children were at school early. They offered to help. The boys asked, "Can we still play Sunflower this Friday?"

"Oh, yes, although I'm not sure what we'll be up against. They have a high school, but I told the principal we'd only play boys in the eighth grade or below."

The girls wanted the experience of riding with the boys in the truck, and because of my sore arm this was a good time.

When we arrived at Sunflower we learned their players would be seventh and eighth graders. "For some reason these boys don't get excited about baseball until they're in high school," the teacher explained. "They haven't practiced much."

Sunny Slope boys were small, but skilled in batting and running. As our score climbed the rooters for Sunflower called us "Sloppy Slope." What did we care? We won. Although the host team lost they didn't show any hostility. Both schools felt it was an afternoon of fun and sports.

The eighth graders and I spent many hours helping Alma prepare for the four tests she was to take in May.

One afternoon as Virginia was ready to leave she put her hand over her mouth. "Oh, I nearly forgot! Mamma wants to see you."

"Do you know why?"

"No, but she'd like to see you this evening."

I never knew quite what to expect from Mrs. Garlow so I hurried through my after-school chores. Tension increased as I drove to their farm.

"Steady, Treva," I cautioned as I approached the house.

Mrs. Garlow met me at the door and stepped out on the porch. Without any salutation she began, "It's time to think about next year so I went to see the Hartzes yesterday."

Oh, here it comes. Stay calm.

"We want you to return for another term if you will."

Relief!

"I'd like to very much." My legs trembled. "This is good news. I've really enjoyed my year."

"We're sorry we can't give you a raise, but these are hard times." She looked into the distance. "We'll be lucky to make ends meet. Prices for crops are down. Many of us will have a difficult time earning enough to eat and pay taxes."

I nodded in agreement. "These are practically the same words I've been hearing at home. Dad and Mother worry too. I feel fortunate to have a job and earn a hundred dollars a month."

Mrs. Garlow smiled and gave a sigh. "I'm glad you're satisfied. You've been a good teacher and handled the job well. Your contract will be ready when you pick up your last check."

There was a lilt in my voice when I said, "Thank you very much." I hurried to my car and drove to the Hartz farm.

After Alma learned she'd passed the four tests that put the whole school in a joyful mood to prepare for the last day of school. Thursday the pupils stacked their books on the shelves at the back of the room and took their personal articles home.

To our dismay, it rained Friday morning. This spoiled our plans to play games and eat lunch in a pasture where a brook gurgled as it meandered through the lush grass. We had to stay indoors.

We played "Who am I", "Who touched me?" and "Where am I?" until the boys decided they'd have an arithmetic match with the three older girls.

90

It was a noisy hour, but none of the boys could solve problems as quickly and accurately as the girls. Mary tried to soothe the hurt she saw in her brothers and friends.

"Don't forget we're a grade or two ahead of you."

"You didn't beat us by much," Harry said. "So don't go home and brag."

"I won't. Next year you can be the smart Snider."

The mothers sent salad, sandwiches and desserts for lunch. Three of them came to help serve. The children sat at their seats and grumbled because the rain spoiled their picnic.

By two everyone was ready to leave. I shook hands with the older pupils when I gave them their report cards and hugged the younger ones. Mary, Katherine and Virginia stayed to help store the equipment and books.

As Katherine walked down an aisle she pointed to something on the floor under a desk. "Ugh! Look at this mess."

We hurried to her side to stare at a pile of potato salad. Then we looked in and under other desks.

Mary put her hands to her head and laughed. "Gee, what a job we're going to have."

Katherine looked rueful. "While we were eating, Reuben asked what the dirty Barretts brought. Maybe I shouldn't have told him."

We ended up scraping and washing potato salad from the shelves of nearly every desk, but an hour later the room was clean and everything stored.

I hugged and kissed each girl in turn. "Have a good summer. Although I won't be your teacher I'll see you this fall."

I smiled with pride as I heard them say:

"It's been a great year."

"You were a swell teacher."

"We sure had a lot of fun this year."

There was joy and sadness on the last day of school, but I would see my friends again in September.

When I picked up my check from Mrs. Garlow she asked, "What are your plans for this summer?"

"My sister Dorothy and I are going to summer school at Chadron. She's only sixteen and the valedictorian of her class. She'd like to teach this fall."

"You must be proud of her. That's an early age to graduate and remarkable she's the smartest in her class.

"I hate to cast a shadow, but I doubt any district will hire her because of her age."

I smiled. "We'll see after she earns these twelve units. She's already passed those terrible seventeen state tests required for a teacher's certificate."

Mrs. Garlow shook my hand. "I wish the best for your sister. Do have a good summer."

THE SECOND YEAR
AT SUNNY SLOPE

Dad took Dorothy and me to Chadron the first week in June. We roomed at the Stratton home and they seemed happy to see me again and to meet Dorothy. Mr. and Mrs. Stratton and I reviewed the last summer's conversation about truckers and railroads. Now the topics were capital punishment and whether or not the Philippine Islands should become independent.

Henry came to Chadron to help me celebrate my twenty-first birthday. He brought three boxes of chocolates he'd won on a punch board.

"They only cost a nickel for each one. I can afford to give them away. Happy birthday to you."

As I held them I kissed him. "Of course you aren't admitting how many nickels you spent when you didn't get anything." I tapped my cheek. "Don't I get a little peck for my birthday?"

He laughed and kissed me.

"This evening some of my friends are having a picnic to help me celebrate. It's at the state park six miles from here." I handed the boxes back to him. "If it's all right with you we'll share the candy with them, but I won't tell how little it cost. They might think it's no good."

He shrugged his broad shoulders. "Tell them. Then you will have more for yourself. Some people don't know it's hard times."

"I'd rather share it. I've been telling them what a great guy you are and this would help to convince them."

Twenty of us attended the party. We enjoyed wieners, buns, potato salad and lemonade. One friend brought a homemade cake. Before the evening was over the candy was gone.

A week after the party Dorothy and I returned to our room from classes to find a letter from Mother. She wrote Dorothy had been chosen as queen of the flower show that would be held the last Tuesday in August.

"The whole campus is going to know about this," I exclaimed. "I'm going to tell President Elliott so he'll announce it next Tuesday at the assembly before you give 'The Three Little Pigs' in Spanish."

Dorothy glared. "Oh, no you won't. If you do, I'll not be on the program."

"All right, all right! But if that were me I'd sure tell everyone."

Dorothy laughed. "You probably would, but I'm not you."

"I'd like to know if there are any other students here who could tell a story in a foreign language. You were lucky to have such a good high school Spanish teacher."

"Yes, I guess I was."

She didn't say anymore, but I knew she was pleased I was so proud of her.

Dorothy excelled in everything she did. The English instructor gave an assignment to write about capital punishment. Dorothy wrote one paragraph opposing the death sentence and received an A. My full page in favor earned only a B+.

I wasn't surprised as Dorothy had always had the talent of expressing herself whether verbally or in writing.

After that there were just more classes and study until Dad came after us the middle of August.

On the way home he filled us in on the plans for the flower show. "You'll wear a long white formal that one of the attendants to the queen of the Aksarben wore last October in Omaha. Your mother and Helen will tell you more."

I looked back at Dorothy who was riding in the back seat. "I just have to laugh about you being dressed so elegantly. When Mother made a dress for you, she had a terrible time getting you to stand still while she measured the length for the hem.

"I remember once you told her if you could just wear overalls, neither of you would have to waste so much time."

"Oh, be quiet."

When we reached home Mother and Helen talked on and on about the coming event, while Norman seemed to see no reason for all the fuss.

"Dorothy earned this recognition. It's only logical she should be the queen. When has any sixteen-year-old been valedictorian of this high school?"

Mother said, "Not everyone agrees with you, Norman. When I met with the planning committee I overheard one lady say to another 'It's a shame it's a girl from the country.' I had to bite my tongue to keep quiet."

The following Monday I drove Dorothy to several school districts where there were vacancies. She was told by the board members they considered her too young. One said, "Come back next year when you're seventeen."

"Are you telling those farmers you were valedictorian of your high school graduation class? And that you will be the flower queen?" I asked.

"No. They aren't interested in things like that. They just want an older and experienced teacher." She shrugged. "I'll help harvest the spuds and husk corn."

The last Tuesday in August, the day of the flower show finally came. The lovely lace-over-satin white formal fitted Dorothy perfectly. I had never seen her look so pretty.

The ceremony began at eight o'clock on the lawn of the Scottsbluff High School. The platform was decorated with award winning bouquets.

Dorothy was escorted by the mayor to a chair in the center while her attendants dressed in long organdy dresses of pastel shades, stood behind her. Those girls were selected because they had the highest grades in the freshman, sophomore and junior classes.

The mayor expressed his delight in the interest shown by both the town and farm committees.

Then he turned to Dorothy. "I have a surprise for you. It appears you have an admirer from the far off Philippine Islands. He is a sailor in the U.S. Navy, stationed aboard the U. S. steamship New York." He then read a telegram from Marion Younghiem, Dorothy's friend. "I regret I cannot be with you today to see you in all your glory." The mayor stooped to pick up a box that held a dozen red roses. "These roses are also from Mr. Younghiem. You must be as special to him as you are to all of us."

Dorothy stood and accepted the bouquet, tears filled her eyes. She bowed to the audience who applauded as they, too, rose from their chairs.

It was a great day not only for Dorothy, but for the whole Adams family.

On the first Monday in September twenty-three boys and six girls welcomed me back at Sunny Slope. The boys practiced football. They didn't seem as excited as they had the previous year because we didn't know another school to challenge.

School had been in session two weeks when eight-year-old Benny came earlier than usual one morning. "Are you all right?" he asked.

"Of course." I was touched, but surprised by his concern for me. "Why do you ask?"

"Don't you know what happened to the teacher at Derrick Creek School?"

"No. Tell me."

Benny spoke rapidly. "She spanked a bad boy. Yesterday morning his older sisters came to school and beat her up. They took off her clothes and set them on fire. She jumped in her car and left." His eyes squinted as though he were trying to view the scene. "Miss Adams, I just want you to know if anyone tries to hurt you, I'll fight 'em."

I leaned over and hugged him. "Thank you, Benny. I'm sure you would. I don't worry about having any trouble. You are all good children."

I felt so lucky that I seldom had a problem. I wondered if this would be the end of that girl's teaching career and pitied anyone who would attempt to handle that school.

During recess and noon the pupils discussed the trouble at Derrick Creek. They said no one would think of treating me that way.

Harry said, "You shake us sometimes, but only when we got it coming."

Until then I hadn't thought about how I'd punished the pupils. But Harry was right. I did shake them. I'd rock them back and forth until the screws came out of the runners that held the desks in place. Then I'd give the mischief-makers screw drivers and have them tighten the screws again.

My brother suggested I should do what his fifth grade teacher had done. Miss Glassy drew three circles on the blackboard in a horizontal line, one for the pupil's nose and the other two for the thumbs when the arms were out-stretched. After five minutes it was difficult to keep the thumbs in the circles. If Miss Glassy saw the arms go down she pushed the pupil's head against the blackboard. Sometimes it caused nosebleeds. After a few boys were punished in this way she didn't have any more discipline problems. I thought about Norman's suggestion, but decided my way was better.

Alma Barrett tried to help as she had seen the eighth grade girls do the year before. She was quiet and the younger children liked her. Most of the time her clothes were clean and she obviously took pride in combing her light brown hair that brushed her shoulders. I thought about giving her some of my sister Dorothy's out-grown dresses, but decided it might embarrass her.

I often wondered why Betty didn't follow Alma's example by keeping clean. I noticed the sisters didn't cling to each other as they did the previous year. Betty's hair was so dirty it became matted and looked as though it were never combed. Soon it would be necessary to have the windows closed to keep out the cold. For this reason I knew something had to be done about Betty's body odor.

When I received my first check at the end of September, I bought new clothes for Betty. On the following Monday I asked her, "Would you like to stay after school today? I want to talk to you."

A cloud seemed to cross her face.

I hurried to explain. "You haven't done anything wrong. I think you'll be happy if you stay. Just tell Alma you'll be late."

"All right," she said without enthusiasm.

Throughout the day I noticed Betty watching me, but I didn't give any hint as to what I had in mind. After the other children were gone I said, "I know your father doesn't make much money, and that Alma gets more new clothes than you. Last Saturday I bought you some new underwear and stockings." I watched her, wondering if she would accept or reject my gifts. She stood with her head bowed so I hurried on. "Also I'd like to give you two dresses my younger sister has outgrown. Would you let me wash your hair and give you a bath before you go home? You can put on clean clothes and surprise your family."

Betty continued to look at the floor without any outward expression. I was almost ready to give up when I noticed she opened her mouth a little and ran her tongue over her lips. Finally she looked at me. "It has been quite a while since I washed my hair. I guess it needs it."

I felt relieved as I didn't know what I'd have done if she'd refused my offer. "I'm so happy to hear you say that."

I hurried to my car to get a big dishpan I'd borrowed from Mother in anticipation. Then I filled the water bucket at the pump near the front door, poured the water into the pan and set it on the stove to heat.

Betty helped with the janitor work while the water heated.

After the chores were finished I dipped my hand in the water to test the temperature. "It's just right, now let's make you beautiful."

When she removed her dress, I saw a ragged, dirty, grey slip. I smiled and said, "It's a good thing I bought a couple, isn't it?" I took the new undergarments from a paper bag.

Her eyes opened wide. She nodded as she looked at the white cotton slips and underwear. The stockings were black like the ones she had on.

I gasped when I saw her one-piece underwear. No amount of washing would have ever made it wearable. Not only was it torn, but it was nearly the color of the stove. Without giving it a second thought I opened the door of the stove and threw the garment into the fire.

As she watched it go up in flames she whispered, "It has been a long time since I changed."

I set the pan of warm water on a desk, gave her a bar of Ivory soap and a washcloth. "I'll wash your back if you'd like." I watched her with compassion as she scrubbed her elbows and heels, which didn't come clean.

Her bath completed, she put on the new undergarments.

I changed the water twice when she washed her hair. After the second rinsing it glistened. While she dried and combed it, I went to the car and brought in the dresses. I held them up. "Would you like to wear one home?"

Her eyes sparkled and she gasped. "Oo-oh, pretty." She fingered them. "No." Tears ran down her cheeks. "I'll wear one tomorrow." She brushed away the tears and smiled.

Since her hair was still damp, and because she had extra clothes, I took Betty home. I felt a bit apprehensive at what I'd done, so decided to make a report to Mrs. Garlow, hoping she would approve of my actions.

To my relief Mrs. Garlow laughed. "Last summer when I took the school census I asked Mrs. Barrett how old Betty was. The mother looked up. There sat the girl on the rafter above my head without a stitch of clothes on. 'I'm eleven,' she said. From what you say about her underwear she must have been airing it, thinking that would have the same effect as washing."

"Thank you for approving what I did. I figured the other pupils and I couldn't be cooped up with that terrible odor all winter. Maybe she'll be a better student. It seems Alma works harder since she keeps herself clean."

The next morning the older boys looked at Betty as though they couldn't believe she was the same girl. When they saw her coming they didn't walk to the far side of the room. A couple of them gave her a shy smile. I noticed there was a jaunty tilt to her head as she offered to help the younger pupils play a game at recess. Betty-dirty had become Betty-pretty.

After my experience with Clyde and the marbles the previous year, I decided to organize a Good Citizen Club. It might enable the pupils to help me if a situation similar to that would arise again and it could help teach them to control their emotions and actions. The club met the last Friday of each month after the last recess. The officers and members planned special activities such as games, hikes and refreshments. Everyone had to be in good standing to participate.

In late October when eleven-year-old Ralph enrolled, I faced a new problem. He craved attention and would do almost anything to get it.

One morning he came wearing new boots. He tramped across the room and out the door. After several trips, I stopped him. "Why are you going outdoors so often?"

"I got to spit. I got somethin' in my throat."

All day long he continued to distract the students, so the next morning I placed a coffee can filled with sand by his desk.

"What's this for?"

"I didn't want you to wear out your boots going outdoors to spit. It might make your throat worse. Now you have your own spittoon."

It didn't take long for his health to improve, but he continued to cause a lot of trouble. He started fights, wouldn't take turns in games, enjoyed making the smaller children cry and talked aloud without permission.

A few days before the club meeting, Ralph broke a toy wagon. So that Friday the first order of business was to exclude him. He was told to sit in the far corner with his face to the wall. No one spoke to him when school was dismissed.

The following Monday he demanded. "Miss Adams, make 'em let me back in the club."

"I can't. You broke the rules. It's up to the club to invite you to join again."

Ralph talked to the president who called a special meeting. It was decided if Ralph brought another toy and didn't get into any more fights, he could rejoin.

When he came one morning in November to tell us he was moving, we sincerely regretted it. Ralph had learned he received much more attention when he became a better citizen and it was the kind of attention he wanted. We told him how much we'd miss him and he seemed to appreciate our sorrow at his leaving.

December was upon us and it was my turn to complain. Most Christmas plays needed as many girls as boys and at this date there was only Alma, Betty and Esther.

I presented our predicament to the pupils. "I don't know how we're going to have a satisfactory program. I can't find a good play that needs only two older girls. Do any of you have a bright idea?"

"What do you mean?" Donald asked.

"We need some boys who will take girls' parts. It's as simple as that."

The children snickered. I waited a few seconds. "Think about it. I really hate to disappoint your parents."

Donald looked at the boys on either side of him before he raised his hand. "I'll be a girl. What do you want me to do? Mamma will make some clothes for me. She's always wanted a girl."

"Wonderful. Thanks for offering. You're a good sport." I heard chuckles. "If we could have another volunteer I've an excellent play called *The Christmas Detectives*. This program could go down in history as one of the best ever given at this school."

There were more snickers. The boys looked at each other. Some slid down in their seats, a few shuffled their feet. I was ready to give up when Harry boldly announced, "I'll be a girl. I guess it won't hurt me."

The boys continued to laugh, but I sighed with relief. "Good! You and Donald will no doubt be the stars of the evening."

Seven-year old Clifford raised his hand. "What do they have to do to be girls?"

"It'll be easy. We'll borrow some ladies' wigs. They can roll up their pant legs and wear girls' coats."

Before school was dismissed our complete program was planned. The children left in a happy mood.

Two weeks before the event we decorated the school. Pupils brought strings of cranberries and popcorn to trim the tree that was a bit larger than the one the previous year. We practiced the program every day after the last recess.

Since Raymond Hartz had been Santa for a number of years I decided to give him a rest. I asked Henry to fulfill that duty.

"The program should have been on the sixth. That's when St. Nicholas visits children in Holland. Can you find me a white horse to ride?"

"Oh, Henry. You're a U.S. citizen now. You're an American and you'll make an excellent Santa."

Henry patted his stomach. "Do you think I'm fat enough?"

"Nearly. One pillow will make you just right and if you stick to 'ho, ho, ho,' I doubt anyone will recognize you."

"All right. I never was a Santa. I might enjoy it enough that I'll change my occupation."

Finally the eventful evening arrived. Soon after seven o'clock every desk had an occupant. Young folks leaned against the back wall while the children sat on the floor.

Pupils who wore costumes crowded into the entry hall. There was subdued laughter as I heard, "Ted, you look just like my grandfather."

"Oh, how-do-you-do, Harriett. It's nice to have a new girl at our school. Too bad Harry isn't here to see you."

"Watch out, Donna. Your hair looks a little lopsided and pull up your stockings. Those garters cut from inner tubes aren't much good."

Everyone quieted when Clifford began his welcome:

> Hello, everyone!
> We are glad you came.
> We're all set for Christmas,
> Hope you are the same!
> Let's all just keep trying
> To bring someone cheer,
> Then we'll have a jolly start
> For a fine New Year.

Alex turned on the wind-up victrola. The audience listened to "Silent Night" and watched five small boys wearing angel costumes their mothers made from old sheets, pantomiming this beautiful carol. No girls could have done better and from the sound of applause when the boys left the stage, others must have agreed.

Esther and four boys presented "Deaf Uncle Sim." The guests laughed when Ted appeared wearing a grey wig made from a new string mop. He sat expressionless while three boys discussed what a rich, old tight-wad this deaf uncle was. When their mother appeared and greeted her brother in a normal

100

tone of voice the boys learned that this was not the deaf uncle. Such a shame just before Christmas!

Next Albert came on the stage carrying a book. He flopped into a chair and appeared to be studying. He looked up and said, "I'm not going to learn this piece. It might hurt my brain."

A call came from off stage. "Tom, are you studying that piece?"

"Yes, but I ought to get a bicycle, or even an airplane to pay for learning it, and that isn't the worst. I've got to stand up there before a bunch of giggling girls. I won't do it."

He threw the book across the stage.

Again he heard, "Tom, now you study that piece."

He quietly walked over and picked up the book. "I'm a martyr, that's what I am."

As the curtain closed he was studying.

The curtain opened again and eight boys carrying large stars made of cardboard and edged in tinsel marched to John Phillip Sousa's recording of "Stars and Stripes Forever."

At recess they had pranced over the schoolyard carrying sticks or long weeds as they practiced the drill. I wondered if they thought of themselves as soldiers.

The Christmas Detectives ended the program. When Betty, Alma, Harry and Donald appeared carrying baskets, the audience giggled. Soon they quieted as the girls told of the plan to take gifts to the home of a poor family that was away for the evening. Donald accidently bumped into Harry and both their wigs moved sideways. I was proud of them when they straightened their false hair and remained serious.

After the girls left the stage William and Alec entered. William picked up a note and read it aloud, "Meet us on the street below the schoolhouse at eight o'clock. We'll break into the house and do our mischief."

Alec grabbed William's arm. "I've always wanted to be a detective. Let's handle this instead of telling the police."

The next scene showed confusion when the six characters met inside the home of the poor family. It ended as the two boys offered to hurry home to get other gifts.

The audience clapped and clapped. Then the names "Harriett" and "Donna" came loud and clear. The applause continued until the boys reappeared and took a bow. They really were the stars of the evening.

Santa entered just as the boys hurried to the hall to remove their wigs and roll down their pant legs.

"Who is that?"

"Raymond is here, so it ain't him."

101

"He sure makes a good Santa!"

"Look at the little kids. They really believe it's the old fellow himself."

Henry said, "Ho! Ho! Ho!" every time he handed out a bag of candy and nuts. Sometimes he patted children's heads. If anyone recognized Santa he didn't admit it. There was a cheery good-bye when the jolly old man left.

As Raymond Hartz munched on a sandwich he commented, "It looks as though I've lost my job. It sure was a swell program. I'll say those two boys who took girls' parts were good sports."

Marion added, "What about the boys who were in the pantomime. I've never seen boy angels before."

Mrs. Beebe, Donald's mother, told a friend, "I couldn't believe he offered to be a girl. He acted as though he enjoyed this part. I was very proud of him."

Mrs. Foreman smiled. "Bently was as pleased as could be when he came home to say he was going to be an angel. Miss Adams knows how to get the most out of our children."

It pleased me that the program was such a success. The happy families left for their homes, "Merry Christmas" and "A Happy New Year" echoed over and over.

HAPPY AND SAD TIMES

Winter and spring can drag on for children unless they have special activities. I was most concerned about the five boys in the seventh grade and the two in the sixth. They had been disappointed we couldn't challenge another school in football and basketball.

One afternoon in January I went to a small town seven miles west of Sunny Slope to contact the manager of the theater. He was changing the marquee when I parked. I explained that I had a good group of boys and that I'd like to bring them to the movies.

"Mister, I know when kids become twelve they're supposed to pay full price. Five are already twelve, but I'm sure they can't afford to pay more than fifteen cents. If I bring them on an evening when you have the fewest patrons, would you let them in on children's tickets.?"

He looked from me to my Model-T coupe. "How are you going to get 'em here?"

"In that," I said, proudly pointing to my car.

He looked at me as though he thought I were kidding.

"Do you think you can get seven kids in your coupe and still have room for yourself?"

"Yes, and I've already made arrangements with the manager of the filling station across the street to stay open until after the show. He'll close the car doors after we get in."

The gentleman scratched his head and laughed. "I've never heard the like. No teacher of mine ever took me to the movies." He looked at me as if he couldn't believe what I was saying. "If you can teach kids all day and help entertain them in the evening, I guess I can contribute a little to the cause. If you bring them on Thursdays, they can get in for fifteen cents apiece, but I'll have to charge *you* thirty-five. It's fifty cents on weekends."

"Oh, that's all right. I'm down to three girls now, but I have twenty-seven boys and I've got to keep them happy."

"I change movies twice a month. I figure in two weeks everybody who's coming will be here by then," he said as I started toward my car.

The next morning I told the boys about the arrangements. They jumped up and down, hugged each other and stared at me.

"Whoopee!"

"Really?"

"You think of the best things."

"When do we start?"

"Next week if your parents agree."

The following Thursday I picked up Albert at six-thirty. He lay on the ledge behind the seat because he was the smallest. William and Alec were next to get in. They were comfortable until we stopped for the twins, then Alex sat on William's lap and Douglas on Donald's.

After Douglas adjusted himself he put his hand on his head. "Take it easy, Miss Adams. Hit the ruts carefully, my head nearly touches the top."

"Do you think there's room for Harry and Alex?" William asked. "This seat sure isn't very wide."

"Of course. We'll just be cozy."

An older brother pushed the Snider boys in. "Ugh!" Harry exclaimed when Alex sat on his lap.

As the brother shut the door he called, "Don't breathe until you get there. If you do you'll force the doors."

From then on unless the dirt roads were too deep in snow we never missed a good movie. Our favorites were *Thief of Bagdad* starring Douglas Fairbanks, *The Gold Rush* with Charlie Chaplin, *The Virginian* with Gary Cooper in the lead, and Tom Mix in *Stage Coach Drive*. But the one we liked best was *Tom Sawyer* starring Jackie Coogan. All the boys expressed a desire to see it again.

"Miss Adams, we'd never get to see these movies if it weren't for you," William said one evening. "Our dad doesn't approve, but he didn't want to tell you."

"I'm glad you get to go. I'm enjoying them too. It's given us something to look forward to. Now if you fellows pass those tests we'll say it's been a good year."

It seemed February came in a hurry. On Valentine's Day Henry took me to dinner. While we were finishing the meal he said, "Well, I think it's time I give you a ring."

"A ring?" My voice rose. I felt my face getting hot. "You have a ring for me? Where is it? May I wear it?"

"Ya, a ring." He reached into his pocket and pulled out a small box. He didn't offer to open it, he just held it. "I want to tell you something." He put his finger beside his nose. I'd seen him do this so many times when he contemplated how to express himself. "This is only a little diamond. If you don't change your mind you'll get a big one when we get married."

"What do you mean?" I frowned in consternation.

He shrugged. "I don't take chances any more. Once I was cheated. I won't let it happen again. I gave a girl a big diamond. She changed her mind. All I have is a dresser scarf she made for me."

I didn't want the evening spoiled by asking about the girl, so I joked, "You lost some money on that deal, but look what you're getting instead. Me!"

He took the ring from the box, placed it on my finger, leaned across the table and kissed me on the lips. When he settled back in the chair his big blue eyes grew larger as he watched me.

I held my hand up, sideways, laid it on the table, made a fist, spread my fingers apart to watch the diamond sparkle. It was so beautiful!

"When do you think we'll get married?" My heart was still palpitating.

"That is up to you."

"What do you mean?"

"I know you want to teach one more year and you need the money to buy the furniture."

I put my hands up to my face in surprise. "I do?" I gulped.

"Ya," he said in a very matter-of-fact voice. "I have bought the farm. It is up to you to buy the furniture."

Although I was stunned by Henry's blunt statement, I respected his ability to manage money and above all I loved him. I moved uneasily. "Then I'd better start saving. I've about two hundred dollars now. Good thing you warned me."

"You have a good start. I'm sure you will manage." He leaned across the table and kissed me again.

I could hardly wait to show the ring to my family. Dad held my hand. "It looks as though you've got him hooked."

Dorothy grinned. "When do I call you 'Missus?' "

"Someday. I'll tell you in plenty of time so you can buy me a wedding present."

I held up my hand and wondered what kind of wedding band Henry would select to go with the larger diamond he promised.

When March roared in like a lion with blustering snow and a strong wind old-timers predicted the month would go out like a lamb, indicating an early spring.

As Alma shook the snow from her long coat she announced the family

105

planned to move because their father had a different job. I had become fond of the three children and was sad they were leaving.

A few days later as we ate lunch the boys expressed a desire for some new playground equipment, but the district had no funds for what was classified as unessential.

That evening I discussed the subject while we ate supper. "What would you think about a box social?"

"Good idea," Dad Hartz said. "Fred Petch, who's a professional auctioneer, would probably sell the boxes. He gets a lot of business from the farmers in this community. I'll ask him."

I was elated. "Wonderful. Marion, what will we do for entertainment? You know I only have one girl, Esther, and I can't ask the boys to take girls' parts again."

She beamed. "Leave that to me. That's right up my alley."

Marion contacted a number of young friends so two evenings each week for a month a dozen came to school to practice.

The night of the social they entertained with a vocal quartette, a harmonica solo and a ukulele duet. The program concluded with a square dance demonstration by two sets of dancers. Abe called while the victrola furnished the music.

About thirty women and girls brought decorated boxes with each holding two suppers. Some of the boxes were covered with flowers made from crepe paper, others resembled objects. Mine was a replica of a covered wagon with the sign "Pike's Peak or Bust!" Marion's was like mine only on hers it read "Busted."

Henry came, but I refused to tell him which box was mine. He bid on Marion's until he paid ten dollars. William bought mine for sixty cents.

When Henry had the opportunity he whispered, "Why didn't you tell me which one was yours? Then I wouldn't have to spend so much money."

I laughed. "Didn't you notice every time you began to bid, the other fellows raised your bid fifty cents? It wouldn't have made any difference which one you tried to get, it would have cost you. Besides, the school needs your money."

That evening the community enjoyed being together for a social event which raised seventy-four dollars. There was more than enough to purchase a merry-go round and some baseball gloves.

One morning after the social Esther brought a note from Katherine asking me to spend the night with her.

When I arrived she greeted me with, "Dave and I are going to be married next February and you're the first one outside our family to know."

I hugged her. "My very best wishes to both of you. With all your experience of helping your mother you should be an excellent wife and some day a good mother."

She extended her hand for me to admire her engagement ring that had a setting much larger than mine. I laid my hand beside hers. "Henry gave me this on Valentine's Day. We'll be married the last of May a year from now."

Katherine squeezed my hand. "I'm so happy for you. I like Henry."

It was a pleasant evening in the Lind home. I helped with the dishes and by ten o'clock all went to bed. Katherine and I continued to talk and laugh until Mr. Lind pounded on her door. In a stern voice her ordered, "Go to sleep. It is time for this household to be quiet."

By April spring was bursting out everywhere. It was on one of these bright mornings that Donald asked, "Do you like to fish?" He hopped from one foot to the other. "Douglas and I caught a mess of perch and bullheads in the irrigation ditch west of our place last Saturday. Would you like to go with us sometime?"

"I sure would. It sounds like fun."

"Could you go this Saturday?"

I made a quick mental inventory of my plans for the weekend. "Yes, if we go early and if I don't stay too long."

"Good, we've a coffee can nearly full of earthworms. There's scads of them in our garden. Mamma said we can have a fish fry for breakfast."

I patted him on the shoulder. These twins were very special. They always cooperated and I'd never forget how Donald was the first to offer to be a girl for the play.

"It sounds as though you've made a lot of plans. Let's hope the fish don't spoil them."

Promptly at seven o'clock on Saturday morning I arrived at the Beebe home. We walked a half mile to the ditch. The meadow larks were singing, a few ground squirrels scurried across our paths, and a young jack rabbit darted in and out among the tall grasses as though he were running a race with us.

When we reached our destination we saw fish jumping out of the water. Douglas caught the first one, but that was the end of his luck. In less than a half hour I'd caught seven.

One time Donald's cork bobber went under. "Whoppee, I've hooked a big one," he yelled. Douglas and I stood watching as Donald pulled the line. Soon his merriment ceased when a large weed appeared.

"We'll let you eat that one all by yourself," Douglas teased.

I looked at my watch. "Boys, I believe we'd better call it quits. I have a lot of things to do today." I pulled my string of fish from the net in the water and held them up. "I'm sorry you didn't get any this time, Donald. Better luck next time."

Donald shrugged. "That's all right. I'm glad you got some. But I can't talk about the one that got away."

While the boys cleaned the fish on a wooden table in the yard, Donald told his mother, "I sure was happy Miss Adams was lucky. Boy, did she get excited. You should have heard her yell. Guess the fish couldn't hear her because the water going over the spillway makes a lot of noise."

"I'm not a school teacher today. I'm just a fisherman having a good time."

As we enjoyed the breakfast Mrs. Beebe said, "I'm sure the boys will always remember the day their teacher went fishing with them."

April was a busy month for the five seventh graders. They were preparing for those four state tests. Penmanship gave them the least worry as they had practiced the Palmer Method since the first grade.

Drawing was a skill based mostly on the proper use of vanishing point. The students could make a row of trees or a road disappear in the proper perspective and set furniture in a room at the correct angles.

Although the boys were good in arithmetic, they had difficulty learning how to balance a ledger in bookkeeping, and debits and credits were often in the wrong columns.

In preparation for the agriculture test the boys recognized the different breeds of farm animals and fowls from sketches. They learned the various types of grain by their blades and shapes of the seed heads.

Since Albert, William and Harry's sisters had passed the tests, the boys felt confident they could, too. "I'm as smart or smarter than Virginia," Albert said. "What she can do, I can do better. I'm sure Douglas and Donald will do all right too."

"Same here," the other two agreed.

On the first Friday in May the five went to Mitchell High School to take the tests. The following Monday Albert greeted me with, "I knew more than they asked."

Two weeks later we had the results and the boys passed with flying colors.

There was other good news that week when a one-teacher school in Sioux County, six miles north of Sunny Slope, sent word they wanted to play baseball with us.

Donald and William rode with me while the others rode in Garlow's truck.

"I don't think there's any Indians left in Sioux County," Donald said, "But I've wondered if any important chiefs lived there."

"I've never heard of any," I said. "William, what do you know about Sioux County?"

"I've heard about the dinosaurs found on Cook Ranch and some day I want to go there."

"So would I," Donald and I said in unison. Then I added, "Did you know a skeleton of one is now in the museum at the university in Lincoln?"

"Really?" Donald sounded excited. "I guess I'd better do some reading about this county."

"But not today. We've a baseball game to think about."

When we arrived the teacher, Miss Garrett, and thirty pupils greeted us. She explained they didn't have enough boys and asked if it would be all right for a boy who had completed the eighth grade the previous year to play. Since Dale was no taller than our boys we agreed.

In the very first inning when eight-year-old Reuben on third base attempted to put Dale out, the older boy fell on Reuben's leg. Reuben screamed. I ran and knelt beside him while Miss Garrett held the group back. I tried to comfort the child as he pointed to his left leg. I felt sick at my stomach.

Miss Garrett helped me lift Reuben into my car while the other children climbed into the truck.

As we traveled toward the Lind home I worried what the father's reaction would be. He was walking in the farmyard when we stopped. "Mr. Lind, Reuben has a broken leg. Shall I take him to a doctor or will you?"

He stood motionless for a moment then removed his cap and beat his leg as he expressed his frustration in German. He glared at me and in English said, "*You* caused all this trouble, so *you* take him to Dr. Watson." The father didn't look at his son, but kept his eyes on me. "Now I'll have a doctor bill because of a silly game and it's time for him to begin thinning beets."

Dr. Watson said Reuben's leg was broken below the knee. While he set the bone I held the boy's hand and squeezed his fingers to let him know how sympathetic I felt. The lad didn't shed a tear though his face contorted often as he looked at me. We watched the doctor put on the cast. When it was finished I put both arms around Reuben and held him tight.

"I'm so proud of you," I whispered. "You are so brave."

After the doctor showed Reuben how to use the crutches we were on our way home.

"Papa sure is mad." The voice was low and sad.

"I know and I'm so sorry. You're such a good boy. Don't worry, in a few weeks you'll be all well again."

When we returned to the Lind home Katherine and her mother helped Reuben into the house.

I spent the weekend worrying about the boy, but Monday morning Esther and her brothers assured me he was doing fine.

While we were eating lunch Harry asked if I'd return next year.

"No. I heard Airport School needed a teacher so I'm going there."

Several said, "We'll miss you."

"I'll miss you too, but I want to tell you about that school. It's known as the traveling school."

"Traveling school! What's that? What a funny name," Alex said.

"It has been moved three times."

"Why?"

"Because it followed the children to the location where most of them lived."

"Is it going to move again?"

"I hope not. Anyway, not while I'm there."

It was a week later that I stopped to see Reuben. To my surprise I found the lad in the field on his hands and one knee, dragging his broken leg in a dirty cast as he thinned beets.

I felt like crying when he looked up and smiled.

"Hello. I stopped to tell you that you passed to the fourth grade. I'll send your report card home with William."

"Thanks, Miss Adams. I'm glad I passed."

"I've enjoyed helping you and I promise to write." I wanted to pick him up and hug him.

"Good-bye. I'll miss you." I turned and hurried to my car because I didn't want him to see my red eyes.

Soon it was time to say good-bye to the families at Sunny Slope. They decided to have a picnic at noon. After the lunch the men and students entertained us with a ball game that ended in a tie.

When a mother asked my plans for the summer I said, "Stay home. Since I expect to be married next spring I need to improve my cooking skills."

My experience at Sunny Slope had been interesting and challenging and good-byes are never happy, but there's always anticipation about tomorrow.

AIRPORT SCHOOL—
PREPARATIONS

Mother often said the way to a man's heart was through his stomach and that surely applied to the man I would be preparing meals for in another year. I'd never seen anyone who enjoyed eating as Henry did.

I hadn't learned to cook well because Dad needed me to herd cattle and hoe weeds in the summertime. During the school months I left home before seven-thirty and returned after five.

When the family learned I'd do most of the cooking, their reaction wasn't very encouraging.

"I'll get a large bottle of castor oil the next time I go to town," Dad said dryly.

"And don't forget to buy a supply of Carter's Little Liver Pills!" Norman added.

At first I prepared simple meals so there were few complaints until I made a custard pie. The crust was so tough everyone ate only the filling. As Dorothy passed her plate with the crust intact she said, "This is as good as new. Tomorrow you can fill it with chocolate pudding."

"Don't forget I'm living with you next winter," Helen said. "I don't want to get sick so you'd better watch Mother closer."

"What about *you* learning to cook?" I asked. "A high school junior should know how to prepare food."

"Yes, but *you* need the practice. I'm not getting married."

Making good bread was the biggest challenge. I watched Mother several times before I attempted that task.

"Remember, practice makes perfect. I'm not much on measurements. I just tell by the feel and the texture if I have enough of everything. One of the secrets of good bread is the length of time you knead it. The longer you knead, the lighter the loaf."

111

My pie crusts never turned out as I desired, but the other desserts and the rest of the meals were satisfactory.

Dorothy was anxious to get a teaching position so I took her to schools where there were vacancies. At the first one the board said they wanted an experienced teacher. When we stopped at the chairman's home in the second district, the wife said her husband was working in a north field.

While I sat in my car, Dorothy took off on foot for her interview. She climbed through two barbed wire fences to reach the field where she found the farmer cultivating corn. In half an hour she returned with a big smile.

"Mr. Russell told me anyone who could climb through a fence like I did could handle a bunch of kids. He said he'd convince his wife, who is also on the board, and the third member that I'd be all right for the job."

I held up my hand to stop her. "Now wait a minute. You mean you don't need to see either of them?"

Dorothy shrugged. "His wife saw me when I asked where I could find her husband. He sounded as though he knew what he was talking about, so let's go home."

As I started the motor I said, "All right, if you're sure. I do remember Mr. Russell told you a year ago to come back when you were seventeen."

"He said I could board and room with them and that I'll get sixty-five dollars a month."

When we told the folks Dorothy's qualification for teaching, Dad chuckled. "If I'd known that, I could have been a teacher instead of a rancher. Think of all the fences I've climbed through."

Although Henry had begun as the veterinarian for the Dairy Development Association they later employed him in their factory. He supervised the making of cheese, butter and ice cream and contacted grocery store managers to promote the products.

Henry began work at six and generally was through by three in the afternoon. He always worked six days each week and every other Sunday. The depression had come to the area so he felt fortunate to have a good position with an adequate salary.

In the late afternoon on my twenty-second birthday Henry drove into the yard with a large object wrapped in heavy brown paper strapped to the top of his Dodge coupe.

I watched as he and Norman unloaded the object and carried it into the living room.

"It's yours. Why don't you open it?"

I hurried over to kiss him. Appearing innocent, I asked, "You mean that?"

He tilted his head. "Ya. I paid for it and brought it here. Now you can take off the wrapping."

I took a butcher knife and carefully slit the paper to reveal a beautiful cedar chest. The design on the front reminded me of large cathedral doors.

While I stood admiring it Henry said, "Just remember I have only a dresser scarf to put in it. It's up to you to fill it."

I felt panicky. I hid my face in my hands. I knew I was responsible for the furniture, but I'd never given a thought to the linens. "You mean it has to be full before we get married.?" I hurried to him, sat on his lap, and hugged him.

"Ya. You will stop teaching. You will have no money." His eyes twinkled. "You better get what you need."

I jumped from his lap and put my hands on my hips. "Oh, I'll have money. I expect to raise chickens, ducks, and geese to sell. And the egg money will be mine."

He thought he had me backed into a corner. "Don't forget you have to buy the feed. Eggs are twelve cents a dozen and with this depression the prices won't get better."

I stomped my foot. This Dutchman was not going to buffalo me! "I'm now an expert cook so I'll charge you for your meals."

He held out his hand and drew me back to his lap "Maybe we can make a deal. Anyway, I'll take you to dinner for free tonight. We'll go to the Eagle Cafe. That's the best place in town."

For the rest of the summer I watched the sales for sheets, towels and table linens. Mother gave me a dozen chicken feed sacks that I hemmed for dish towels. Soon the chest was half full.

July slipped by and August meant it was time to think about school. I was looking forward to this new venture when Belle Hays, a member of the Airport School Board came to our house. She and Mother chatted about the year she stayed with us in town when she was a high school senior and I was four years old.

After a few minutes she stopped talking and cleared her throat. "Treva, I came to ask for your contract."

My heart skipped a beat. "What do you mean? Don't you want me for your teacher?" Tears slid down my cheeks. "I don't understand."

Belle twisted her handkerchief. "We can't hire a married woman."

"I'm not married!" I screamed. "I won't be until next spring after school is out." I collapsed in a chair and continued to sob.

Belle walked over and put a hand on my shoulder. "Oh, Treva, don't cry. You don't know how relieved I am to hear this. I was told you were married."

"Then you still want me?"

"Of course. You don't know how I hated to come here."

I stood and squinted my eyes. "I don't know who told you this and I don't want to know." I felt my legs tremble, my voice quivered. "All I can say is that I hate trouble-makers and liars."

Belle nodded and smiled. "Now let's talk about good things."

I heaved a sigh of relief. "I'm ready for that."

"One of the older girls in the neighborhood will clean the school. Jerry will mow the grass and cut the weeds. We'll buy a new stove as soon as we get the tax money. Right now we have about one hundred and twenty-five dollars on hand, but we expect more from the County Treasurer very soon."

I blew my nose. "Did you send for the supplies I'll need?"

"Yes, we ordered them from the University Publishing Company in Lincoln. We'll get the rest from Montgomery Wards."

"Good. I'll be over next Monday to get the school key. I'll be working there all next week."

Belle stood. "Now I must hurry home to tell the good news to Jerry and call the Schaffers."

She told Mother good-bye and I walked to the car with her.

When I drove into the schoolyard the following Monday, my attention was drawn to the belfry where a large bell hung. I quivered with excitement. I could hardly wait to pull the rope to hear it call the children into the classroom.

Next I noticed the big double doors on the west end of the building and recalled Whittier's poem entitled "In School Days."

Part of one stanza reported:

> The feet that, creeping slow to school,
> Went storming out to playing!

Were those wide doors an indication that I'd have an unruly group?

After entering, I passed through the cloakroom and on to the classroom to the teacher's desk. In a large middle drawer was a copy of the school census. The majority of the sixteen boys would be in the third and fourth grades. Eight of the fourteen girls were first and second graders. With this information I felt as though our activities would be somewhat different from those at the previous school.

The classroom had cream colored walls and six windows, three on each side. The blackboard was behind the teacher's desk and the large heating stove was at the opposite end of the room. There were five rows of desks fastened on one-by-fours. On the left, near the wall stood a large cupboard filled with books.

To my surprise and delight there was an old pump organ against the wall to my right. I hoped I could remember to keep pumping the pedals with my feet while I concentrated on playing the music. For the first time I was happy I'd taken piano lessons Mother insisted on when I was a child.

By Friday my preparation for the beginning of school was complete. I wrote "Miss Adams" on the right side of the blackboard and smiled. This would be the last school where I'd be known by that name.

I closed the door, turned the key, and gazed again at the bell I'd ring the following Monday morning.

The Airport School, 1931–32.

In this recent picture of the Airport School the bell has disappeared and the old front door has been moved to the side.

THE FALL OF 1931

August thirty-one appeared to be a very exciting day for the thirty pupils who greeted me on the steps of the Airport School. Among them were three Japanese children. Although there were several Asian families in the county, this was my first contact with them.

"It's so nice to see all of you," I said. "I came early too."

A small boy looked up at me. "Hello, I came to see what you look like."

"What is your name?" I asked, surprised at his frankness.

"Dale."

"Hello, Dale. I hope you like what you see."

He put his head down as though embarrassed that he'd spoken so boldly. After a few moments he looked up and nodded.

As I patted a small child on the head I asked, "Do you know why I came early?"

He and others shook their heads.

I felt a little foolish when I confessed, "I want to ring the bell."

"We're all here. You don't need to," Victor informed me.

I laughed. "That's right, but I want to ring it because I've never rung one before."

The children giggled. They gathered round me when I pulled the rope in the cloakroom to listen as the melodious tones pealed forth.

I turned to Victor's sister, Martha. "Did you hear it last year from your home?"

"Oh, yes. If you'll ring it ten minutes before school starts we'll try to get here on time. All four of us have lots of chores every morning."

"That's a good idea. It might keep some others from being tardy. I'll use the hand bell when it's nine o'clock."

117

Jake Haun said, "I like to hear that big bell and when I grow up I want one in my front yard."

Victor chuckled. "Would you ring it every morning at nine?"

"Maybe."

It was time for the girls to get into one line and the boys in another. We saluted the flag, sang the first stanza of "America" and entered the classroom. In a few minutes everyone was busy.

An hour later a small Japanese boy entered. He announced in a loud voice, "George, Papa wants you."

Without looking at me the older boy joined his brother at the door. My brow lowered in a puzzled frown as I watched in silence while the two left the room. "Harry, why did your brother leave?"

"Our father doesn't speak English. George has to go to the bank with him. He'll come back soon."

School progressed so smoothly the first three weeks, I decided there would be no trouble. But one morning when I came out for recess with the older students, I found the eight little girls crying. My experience in the other schools where the majority of small children were boys didn't prepare me for this kind of problem.

"What's the matter?" I asked.

Tearfully Irene said, "Ida doesn't like me and neither does Joan."

Esther threw her arms around me as she sobbed. "Pauline doesn't like me. She told Mary not to play with me."

One by one the girls told who didn't like them. I was stunned. How would I handle this? Finally I sat on the step and pretended to cry.

"What's the matter, Miss Adams?" Joan asked.

"Eight pretty girls don't like each other. I'm sad."

Joan patted my shoulder. "Don't cry. I'll like my friends if they'll like me."

I stood. "Good." I gazed at each one questioningly. "How about you other girls?"

They looked at each other and grinned. Soon they were holding hands and playing "Ring Around the Rosey."

During the first month Mrs. Southwell mailed health forms to be completed and sent home with the report cards the last of September. To the best of my ability I examined each student's eyes, ears, nose, throat and teeth. Many had cavities and a few were mouth breathers because of swollen adenoids.

Soon after school started I began my monthly trips to the Scottsbluff Public Library to check out thirty books. I encouraged the pupils to read any book that looked interesting whether it was for first graders or their own reading level. A number of them admitted it was the first time they had ever read a book for pleasure.

Each morning and again after the noon recess I read stories aloud. Some of their favorites were *Beautiful Joe, Black Beauty, The Little Lame Prince* and the *Ruth Fielding* series. *Billy Whiskers,* the goat that was always in trouble, gave us the most laughs.

Early in October I spoke to the board members about plans for a Christmas program.

"It sure would help if we could have stage curtains," I explained.

Belle, the treasurer, quickly agreed. "Joan told us you talked about curtains so I checked at Read's Furniture Store. For ten dollars we can buy enough burlap to make them. You go ahead with your plans."

On Monday following Thanksgiving I told the pupils about the program. "Last year the school where I taught had two plays that everyone seemed to enjoy. We also sang, performed pantomimes and drills, and some spoke pieces. Does that sound good to you?"

"Yes! Yes!" They cried in unison.

"Then I'll start this afternoon to read the plays and you can decide which part you want."

A few clapped, some looked at others and snickered. soon all were busy.

After the last recess I began by saying, "I want to tell you something that happened last year. There weren't enough older girls for one play, so two boys volunteered for girls' parts."

Most of the boys looked as though they were about to be sick. "Ugh!" Jake said. "Are we lucky. I sure wouldn't want to be a girl."

When I read "Deaf Uncle Sim," Martha said, "I'd like to be the mother. Mamma has a long black skirt and blouse in her trunk that she brought from Russia. She plans to cut them up and make braided rugs. I know she'll let me wear them."

"Fine. And you'll make a good mother when you scold your children. I think you could do that very well."

Everyone laughed. Victor said, "She's good at that. But who wants to be her kids?"

Despite the threat, most of the smaller boys raised their hands. Jerome and Robert were selected, and Charles would be Deaf Uncle Sim. Six older students planned to present *The Christmas Detectives.*

"Victor, would you give a recitation while pretending you're Santa?"

He looked pleased. "Yes, I guess so, if you can find a suit."

"That's no problem. My mother will make one. You're pretty skinny, but she'll make it roomy and we'll stuff in pillows."

The others giggled. Victor looked disturbed.

119

"Don't pay any attention to them," I said. "Their little brothers and sisters will love you. Bring a clean gunnysack for the toys."

"Will it be at night?" Pauline asked.

"Yes. All the parents will want to see the program."

Several children offered to bring kerosene lamps that would fit into the brackets above the windows. The entertainment would be the last Friday evening before vacation.

I made hand-written copies of the plays by using an indelible ink. Then I pressed the master on a hectograph which was a sheet of clear gelatin in a large pan. It took only a few seconds to duplicate each page, but the whole procedure was long and tedious so I did it in the evening at my apartment.

Most of the pupils spent their free time practicing their parts. Before I left each evening I practiced on the pump organ so I could accompany Martha when she sang "Away In A Manger."

All the pupils had a part in the one hour program. The audience clapped loud and long after each performance.

Mothers had made stockings from red netting and filled them with hard candy and nuts. I asked Henry to be Santa again. He seemed to enjoy it as much as he had the previous year.

Before the adults left they helped to put the classroom back in order. The new stage curtains were pulled to the sides of the room and tied to the wall with pieces of binder twine. It gave me a feeling of great satisfaction that my final Christmas program had been such a success.

WINTER

The pupils returned in a happy mood after a week's vacation. They were delighted that the first big storm of the winter had left a foot of snow on the school yard.

"Miss Adams, may we play 'Fox and Geese' at recess?" Victor asked when he arrived.

"That sounds like fun. Why don't you, Charles, and George go out now and make the circle and paths for the geese and fox to run on? You may be the first fox at recess."

"Good!" he said as he and the other two left the room.

Joan took hold of my hand, "I'd rather make a snow angel."

"All right, you and your friends may do that. Remember when recess is over, use the broom to sweep all the snow off your clothes. I don't want any of you to catch cold."

Irene complained, "But, I don't know how to make an angel."

"That's easy," her friend said, "Just lie on your back in the snow and move your legs out and in a couple of times to make the dress. At the same time make your arms go above your head and bring them down to your sides." She demonstrated the movement. "That makes the wings. When you get up it looks like an angel's been there."

The three first grade boys decided they'd make a snowman. It took all their play periods to roll the balls. At the afternoon recess George and Charles lifted the two smaller snowballs on top of the largest one to form the snowman.

"Pauline, you're tall," Dale said. "Would you put a face on him? Here's three pieces of coal for his eyes and nose."

Martha laughed. "He sure needs a mouth. Whoever heard of a man who didn't like to talk?"

Virgil ran up with a dried weed. "Here, Pauline, I think this looks like a mouth."

"He's got to have arms," Harry said as he brought two sticks about the same length and stuck them in the sides of the middle snowball.

When the children were ready to go home Martha said, "I think I can find an old dishpan for the snowman's hat. He might catch cold if his head isn't covered." She smiled. "This was a good way to start 1932."

Everyone agreed.

The next morning, after the dishpan was set jauntily on to the snowman's head, Charles stood inspecting the results. "He looks exactly like our neighbor. We better name him Mr. Tanner."

Some mornings it was twenty degrees below zero with the temperature rising only a few degrees before noon. On those days we remained inside at recess. The smaller children spent their free time in a sandbox Jerry had made and placed near the stove. The nine second and third graders liked the game of dominoes.

"Miss Adams, will you please play with us?" Irene asked.

"All right, but remember if your sum ends in zero or five and you don't call it out right away, I'll add it on to my score."

"I know," Esther said. "We play this game at home. Papa does the same thing. That's why I can add and subtract quicker now."

"So can I," Ida boasted.

"I've noticed you're both doing better. Let's get started."

The older children liked a card game called "Touring." A large number could enjoy it at one time. The object was to travel two hundred fifty miles to win the game. Each player tried to stop his opponents by giving them cards that read, "Out of gas," "Flat tire," "Detour," "Overheated radiator," and "Needs oil." The players had to show the appropriate cards before they could advance toward their destination.

Soon after the first of the new year I told Belle, "I'll sure be happy when you get a new stove. The grates are getting worse. Chunks of burning coals fall into the ash pan. That's dangerous. Every evening before I leave, I must remove all the coals. It's a hot, messy job."

"I'm sorry it's taken so long to get a new heater. We just received a check from the County Treasurer. Jerry and Roy Schaffer plan to buy a new stove this weekend."

The following Monday a beautiful coal burner replaced the old one. It was a relief to have a warm classroom by the time the pupils arrived. They stood in front of it holding out their hands to absorb the warmth.

"This sure feels good," Pauline said. "That old one never did warm the north side of the room. I was always cold. Hurrah for the new stove!"

Joan brought a note from her mother.

> Dear Treva, the men found this stove at Standard
> Hardware for $89.50. It looks good. If it causes any
> trouble let us know. Belle.

I felt so lucky that I taught in a district where the school board tried to provide everything I considered necessary.

Soon after we got the new stove a kit came that I'd ordered. When assembled it would be a replica of George Washington's home in Mount Vernon. The older children made miniature furniture of cardboard, small pieces of wood and wallpaper.

"Miss Adams, does it snow in Virginia?" Charles asked. "Snow would look pretty around Washington's home."

"I've read in the papers that it's been raining in Washington, D.C., but this year there's been no snow. Since Mount Vernon is just across the Potomac River from the capital I'm sure it hasn't snowed in Virginia."

"Does it ever snow there?"

"Oh, yes, but not this year."

Charles looked up from the chair he was making. "Then let's pretend it's a year when it did snow."

"I have no objections," I said.

I'd read in *The Instructor,* a magazine for teachers, how to make artificial snow by using coal, water, salt and household ammonia.

The recipe worked so well we piled artificial snow around the mansion. Charles decided to put a little on the roof also to make a true winter scene.

We had just completed the project when Mrs. Southwell visited us.

"It's lovely," she said as the children explained what they'd done. "I'm sure President Washington would have been pleased. You've done a very good job."

Then she turned to me. "Would you like to have a student teacher the last week in February? There's a girl in the senior class at Gering High School who would like to be a teacher next year in a one-room school. You always have so many interesting projects to help children learn. I'm sure you could give her many ideas."

I felt honored that the superintendent approved of my teaching ability. "Yes, I'll be happy to help her. I didn't have an opportunity like that before I began. But, I'm not sure it would have helped me because my first school didn't have any standard equipment except textbooks. I just learned by doing."

"Thank you for saying she may come. Isabbell is a petite, vivacious blond who I believe has potential as a teacher. She'll be here the week of the twenty-second."

It made the pupils feel important that their school had been selected to have a student teacher. They were well-behaved, so I had no worry that anyone would try to "Show-off" while Isabbell was there.

After Isabbell had observed on Monday she taught the spelling classes the next day. She appeared confident and patient. When her teacher and Mrs. Southwell visited on Thursday, Isabbell demonstrated her ability. In a capable way she helped the fifth graders understand the multiplication of fractions. Friday she had complete charge of the school.

When four o'clock came I said, "I think you did an excellent job. I liked the way the pupils responded to you. It's so necessary for them to like and respect their teacher."

"Thank you so much. It's been a most rewarding week for me. I hope I can teach as well as you do."

When the children became fourth graders they knew it was time to begin studying for those dreadful state tests. Sometimes while I helped a lower grade I noticed the room became very quiet. The older pupils were obviously listening. Later some of them told me they had never studied that topic before, or they never heard that particular story and sometimes the younger ones listened to discussions in the upper classes.

This helped me to realize that there were some advantages in a one-room school. It also made me feel these children learned to become independent at an early age.

One morning Martha asked, "Can you come to our house tomorrow after school and stay all night? Mamma wants to know."

"I'll be happy to. Thank you very much."

The next day I walked home with Martha. The farmhouse looked as though it had been freshly painted inside and out. Mrs. Propp, wearing a white apron over a blue cotton dress, gave me a warm welcome. "I'm sorry it took so long to get you here," she said.

"I've been busy too. I must congratulate you on the way the children come to school so clean and neat. I notice if Victor or George gets dirt on his clothes he always removes it right away."

The proud mother smiled as she brushed a strand of brown hair away from her face. "I seldom scold. As soon as the children come home, all four change their clothes. The girls have to wear the same dress for a week as they each have only two for school and a good one for church."

Mr. and Mrs. Propp were first-generation Germans who came to America from Russia. Their forefathers left Germany to escape being drafted into the army. The present generation heard life was better here than in Russia. Many came to Scotts Bluff County.

When supper was ready the family lined up against the south wall of the dining room with the two-year-old at one end and the father at the other. The baby, speaking in German, gave her prayer first and each followed with the father giving the longest and last prayer.

Victor, Martha, George, and Esther sat on a long bench at one side of the table. An older brother and sister, little Dorothy, and I sat opposite, while the parents were at the ends.

Mr. Propp had just butchered a beef so we had a tender roast, mashed potatoes, candied carrots and slaw. After we were through eating Martha helped her mother clear the table.

Martha returned carrying the tallest cake I'd ever seen. It was completely covered with whipped cream and topped with cherries and walnuts.

"We call this a torte in the old country," she explained as she set the plate on the table.

"It looks too good to eat."

Martha smiled at me. "She made it especially for you. It's her mother's recipe."

"Then we'd better eat it!" I looked at Mrs. Propp. "Do tell how you made it."

As she cut the torte and placed the pieces on handpainted plates she explained, "Three days ago I baked eight thin, round cakes that I stored in a tight container. An hour ago I placed the first cake on a flat plate, covered it with chocolate pudding, and added another cake which I spread with whipped cream. I continued to alternate the fillings until all eight cakes were stacked. Then I covered it with whipped cream."

Although I knew it wasn't proper I wanted to smack my lips as I ate the delicious dessert.

After supper the girls and I washed and dried the dishes, Mrs. Propp patched overalls, and the boys and their father finished the chores which included milking several cows.

Finally all the tasks were completed. While the children played a game of dominoes the parents and I visited. These first-generation Americans had little difficulty expressing themselves. Although their language was different from Henry's, I noted there was a likeness.

"Someday I hope we'll have enough money so we can hire help," Mr. Propp said. "I hate to keep the children out of school to harvest potatoes and beets. Right now that's the only way we can get the jobs done."

I nodded. "You're in the same situation as my parents were. We children always had to miss two weeks of school to pick potatoes. We didn't raise beets on the ranch."

For about a half hour we discussed our differences and similarities. When it was nearly ten I turned to Martha. "Are you about ready to go to bed?

I must get to school early tomorrow. I didn't finish all my work before I came here tonight."

She yawned. "Yes, I'm ready." Then she went to the kitchen to pick up a kerosene lamp to light our way up the stairs.

One Monday morning George and Jake, who were neighbors and close friends, came to school full of enthusiasm.

"Miss Adams, on Saturday afternoon we had the best time skating on the swamp," Jake said. Everything is frozen over. The ice is like glass. It's really fun going from one pond to the other trying to dodge the cattails!"

George interrupted, "We want to know if the whole school can go skating some afternoon."

Since I'd grown up skating on Lake Alice I tingled with excitement. "I'm sure in favor and I'll ask the school board. Maybe some of them would like to go with us." I paused and my thoughts slipped back in time. "Before I had skates I slid on the ice wearing my overshoes. Do any of you have sleds?"

Three children raised their hands.

"Good. You can take your classmates for rides on the ice."

We decided to go at one o'clock the following Friday if we were given permission. I sent a note home with Joan.

The next morning Belle sent word saying she and Jerry would join us at the swamp. It seemed the children were especially good that week. They studied hard during school time, but talked about the forthcoming excursion at every recess. All the pupils had permission to go.

It was a fifteen-minute walk to the swamp which was near the railroad track and not too far from the airport. Naked willow trees and tall dried swamp grasses bordered the ponds. Two large beaver dams were on the edge of one of them. Most of the cattails had burst open, but their stalks stood like soldiers.

We smelled burning wood, saw smoke curling upward and heard voices as we followed a path to the edge of the swamp. There we found Belle and Jerry busily putting branches on a bonfire.

After greeting us, Jerry took an iron frame from his truck and placed it over the blaze.

"What's that for?" Victor asked, pointing to the frame.

"Wait and see," Jake said in a way that didn't tell us whether he knew the answer or not.

For the next hour the children skated and took sled rides. Only a few had clamp-on skates, but that didn't matter. Everyone slid over the ice one way or the other. They went from pond to pond pulling and pushing each other. Jake and George demonstrated their ability to skate backwards. When Jerry and Belle skated together holding crossed hands, the pupils watched them in awe.

126

After an hour the children returned to the fire. It was burning low.

"Just right," Belle said. Then she went to their truck and brought back a big bag of marshmallows, while Jerry placed a covered can on the iron frame.

The children scurried here and there finding willow sticks so they could toast the marshmallows. Then Jerry lifted the can from the fire. He removed the lid. It was hot cocoa! While each of us held a tin cup he filled it brimming full.

Oh, what a party! None of us could remember a better time. And that party was none too soon because warmer days and strong winds began to thaw the ice and melt the snow drifts. Poor Mr. Tanner, who had guarded our schoolyard for nearly two months, became only a pile of snow by the pump. Spring couldn't be too far away

Katherine and David's wedding

KATHERINE'S WEDDING

Dear Miss Adams,

That day is almost here. This coming Sunday, to be exact. February 28. Yes, it's our big day. David and I will be married at the St. John's Lutheran Church immediately following the regular service.

We're really excited about the musicians who are coming from Ft. Collins, Colorado. The Scheiders have the reputation for being the best wedding orchestra to be found.

I'll see you Sunday.

Your former pupil,
Katherine

Less than two years before, Katherine had completed the eighth grade at Sunny Slope School. I had kept in touch with her through letters. It seemed strange that a former pupil would wed before her teacher. I was eager for Sunday to come.

That morning when I entered the sanctuary I felt embarrassed because the church service was still in progress. I sat in the nearest available pew which happened to be on the men's side. Some women across the aisle stared at me and girls covered their mouths to conceal silent giggles. My cheeks burned. I felt that everyone was looking at me.

The congregation stood for the closing hymn. One old gentleman seated near me fell behind during each stanza. I noted with amusement the others waited for him to finish the verse. After the minister offered a prayer we all sat down.

Soon I heard the melodious sound of an ensemble. The musicians, standing just outside the entrance, played the wedding march from Wagner's

Lohengrin. I turned to watch four-year-old Edna May, the groom's niece, walk down the center aisle scattering rose petals. She was followed by seven couples known as the best girls and the best boys. The girls wore floor-length dresses in pastel shades and the men wore dark suits.

Then Katherine and David advanced toward the altar, hand in hand.

What a beautiful bride! A lace jacket with a small standing collar covered the bodice of the ankle-length white satin gown. The long tulle veil was attached to a halo embroidered with silk flowers and beads. Her white satin slippers were tied with silk bows. She carried a dozen pink rose buds. David, following a European custom of his family, had obviously spared no expense when he purchased his bride's clothes.

The groom in a black suit, white shirt, and black bow-tie had a long white ribbon fastened to his coat lapel. The boutonniere was a pink rose.

There was no further music, only a short ceremony and a prayer spoken in German, their native language. The couple left the church first with the attendants following. For a few minutes I again heard wedding music, then a general state of confusion ensued as the guests rushed to their automobiles. All the cars belonging to the bridal party were gaily decorated with streamers of crepe paper. They headed the procession that led to the farm of the groom's parents.

Upon my arrival, I noticed the living, dining and bedroom furniture had been placed in the yard. It was a blessing the weather cooperated. Otherwise where would they have stored all those household goods for this special day?

I joined the other guests on their way to the back door. David and Katherine stood with their parents on the porch to welcome us.

As I shook hands with the bride and groom they showed me their wedding rings. "You're a charming couple," I said. "I hope you'll always be as happy as you are now." I hugged Katherine and smiled at David.

I walked on through the large, steaming kitchen where six busy women were preparing food. When I entered the next room I saw it had been stripped of furniture to make room for the tables and chairs which would accommodate some of the two hundred guests. Through curiosity I continued to wander into the other rooms. There I visited with a doctor, the banker and a number of persons who managed stores and businesses in the neighboring towns.

About a half hour later Katherine took my hand. "Come with me. You're to sit with us."

She introduced me to the minister and his wife and the fourteen best girls and boys. We sat at a large table with the traditional wedding cake in the center.

A few minutes later a young lady wearing a pretty white apron over her silk dress approached the bridal couple with a pitcher of homemade wine in one hand and a goblet in the other. One after the other drank from the goblet.

With a quickened heart I saw her come toward me. If my mother had only been there, I could have told by her look what I should do. In the first place I'd grown up hearing about the evils of drinking. I didn't know if that much wine would make me sick or drunk. In the second place I kept thinking about everyone using the same glass, and third, if I refused would I offend Katherine. I pretended to sip the wine and handed the glass back. No one seemed to notice.

The first course was a soup with a chicken broth containing homemade noodles and walnut-sized balls. It was so good. I turned toward the girl beside me. "What is in these little balls?"

"This is a special wedding soup," she explained. "The butter balls consist of crushed toast which has been run through the flour sifter. Butter, eggs, cream, and a dash of allspice are added. The ingredients are carefully measured and handled so the dough won't be too tough or fall apart." She paused, then proudly added, "My mother helped make them."

After the soup bowls were removed the girl brought a feast beyond my comprehension. The parents of the bridal couple shared the expense of the food and beverages. They had butchered a steer, a hog, and thirty chickens. Potatoes and carrots were peeled and roasted with the beef. There was plenty of homemade rye bread and fresh coffee cakes called "dinna kucha." The meal ended with a variety of pies and cakes. How the women of the community must have worked to prepare it!

We'd just finished eating when the master of ceremonies known as the "house father" arose. He held Katherine's right slipper high above his head.

"Hear you. Hear you! All seven best boys. What am I bid for this lovely slipper? Do I hear thirty-five dollars to begin with? That will cost each of you a mere five dollars. What am I bid? Ah, I hear twenty dollars. My fine young friends, this slipper was worth more than that before the lovely bride put her toes into it. Come on! Come on! We must get this couple off to a good start. Speak right up and spend your money freely."

After much cajoling the young men finally consented to contribute ten dollars each. Katherine smiled to show her delight as David handed her the slipper and put the seventy dollars into his pocket.

It was now time to open the wedding gifts. I overheard the guests discussing whether this would be a thousand dollar or a two thousand dollar wedding. There were several sets of china, a living room suite, an electric range, and a beautiful carpet. They surely wouldn't have to buy linens or woolen blankets for a long time. My gift was a copy of *The Gleaners* by Jean Francis Millet.

After the presents had all been opened and admired, the "house father" announced it was time for the wedding dance. We followed the bride and groom to the tool shop. It was empty except for crude benches along the walls. When

131

they were filled, the six-piece orchestra started to play. The cooks began to folk dance. I'd never heard such whooping and hollering. Perhaps they were saying German words, but it sounded something like "Hip, hip, hooray!" The cooks danced without partners. The second time around the room each one put her hand into a box to select a piece of china. Raising the dish high above her head she threw it to the floor with such force, the pieces flew everywhere. I shielded my face with my hands. The women continued to dance until the box was empty.

"Why are they doing this?" I asked the girl sitting beside me.

"Several reasons are given," she replied. "I'm not sure which is correct. Some say it breaks the apron strings that bound the couple to their parents. Others say it helps the guests give their money more freely."

I wondered how this activity would get more money for the couple as I watched the ladies sweep the floor. The orchestra began to play a waltz and the bridal couple danced. Soon the cooks joined them. The ladies moved around the room first alone and then with each other, following a custom that had come with them from Europe.

The attendants were next to join the group, then dancing opened to the guests. Anyone wishing to dance with the bridal couple dropped money between the strings of the dulcimer, a popular instrument. This was to help pay for the orchestra. The partners then pinned bills on Katherine's and David's clothes before the waltz or polka began. After each dance friends removed the money and handed it to Katherine who tucked it in the bosom of her dress.

I smiled to myself. If Henry and I were to have a German wedding I wouldn't have to struggle to save for our linens and furniture. Think of all the money we'd have! I watched for quite some time before I had the courage to pin five dollars onto David's coat so I could dance with him.

By late afternoon Katherine's gown could no longer be called beautiful because of the many pin holes and soiled spots where sweaty hands had touched it.

At seven o'clock we returned to the house to enjoy the leftover food from the midday meal. After Katherine cut a piece of the wedding cake and fed it to David, the guests had the rest.

I looked at my watch and with reluctance whispered to Katherine, "I must go."

"Really? We'll dance again until ten. Can't you wait for the late lunch? We serve a special garlic sausage, cheeses and a rye bread."

"I'd like to stay and the food sounds so tempting, but I'd better go." I squeezed her hand. "This has been a wonderful experience. Thank you for asking me." When I kissed her good-bye I promised, "I'll visit you when you're settled in your new home."

"Don't forget." She returned my kiss. "I'll be looking forward to it."

SPRING

Henry decided we'd live on his farm while he continued to work at the cheese factory in Gering. Therefore, when the new renter came the first of March he and his family moved into the hired man's house, leaving the larger one for us.

After the house was empty, I spent every Saturday cleaning, painting and papering. I tackled the kitchen first, painting the walls and ceiling a canary yellow. The spacious pantry with large sugar and flour bins, many drawers and deep cupboards became sparkling white. I'd learned from Mother that attractive wallpaper helped to make a room look livable, so I papered the large room that would be our living and dining area. With the leftover paper I covered the walls of the clothes closet. The last room on the first floor to get my attention was the bathroom which became a pale cream-color.

I moved upstairs from the living dining room to the two bedrooms. I papered both of them. I looked into the closet that extended the full length of the upstairs. Since this would be used only for storage, I cleaned the walls and floor and left it as it was.

Across the entire front of the house was a glass-enclosed porch. This would be used in summer for leisure and dining. I'd asked Mother to make curtains of colorful print for all the windows. We'd put the ice box at the end near the kitchen.

Henry did a great deal of kidding about my dowry. "Wouldn't you feel bad if our friends and family came and they wouldn't have a chair to sit on?" He grinned. "Don't forget we need a bed."

I felt my cheeks burn and looked away. I hoped the six hundred dollars I'd saved would pay for everything we needed. All the floors would be covered with pieces of linoleum or congoleum rugs. The congoleum rug for the living and dining room had a bordered pattern like a wool rug with small designs throughout the center. It would be easy to mop and wax like the linoleum on all the rest of the floors. The coverings would average nine dollars a room. I planned to purchase sturdy, but attractive furniture that would include a three-piece bedroom suite, a davenport and matching chair, a gateleg table and six dining chairs. Before winter came we'd need to buy a coal-burning heating stove for the big room. Mother volunteered to make sheer curtains for all the windows from material I'd purchased for fifty cents a yard.

The former renter sold us the coal-burning kitchen range and a Coleman four-burner gasoline cookstove for twenty-five dollars. I'd need only a worktable, a small dining table and four chairs to complete the kitchen.

The windmill in the corral furnished the power to pump water into a five hundred gallon storage tank. Whenever we needed hot water in the kitchen or bathroom we would have to start the fire in the range. The pipes ran from a fifty gallon tank behind the stove through the firebox.

We'd need three Coleman gasoline lamps to light the house and two lanterns to carry to the other buildings.

I felt confident everything would be in place when we were married in our new home on May twentieth.

March was the time for some pupils to move, too. Charles and his three brothers reported their father had found another job, so they left the district. Two weeks later Mary and George enrolled.

The next day the five Rizenburg children started. They were poorly clothed and their lunches were meager. The youngest had a persistent cough and always had a runny nose. They attended school on the average of three days each week.

The state allowed only twenty days of excused absence per school year. I wondered what the County Superintendent's reaction would be when she received my end-of-the-month report and learned these children had already missed over forty days of school.

A few days later the oldest Rizenburg child, Carol, arrived alone, tears streaming down her cheeks. Between sobs she said, "Papa is in jail. The sheriff came after him yesterday."

I wasn't surprised, but I was deeply moved. "I'm sorry," I said slowly and put my arm around her. "Why have you been absent so much?"

She wiped away the tears. "I don't know."

The next morning she brought a note from her mother.

> Dear Miss Adams, I need help. We got no food.
> Please help us. Thank you. Lena Rizenburg.

I pondered the situation. The term was nearly over and this was the first serious problem I'd encountered. At recess I told Martha and Pauline about the note. Quietly they related the information to the other children. They all decided to bring food.

The next morning Belle came to take potatoes, eggs, a two-pound slab of home-cured bacon, home-canned peaches, a head of cabbage, a few carrots, jars of milk, flour and sugar to the destitute family.

Two weeks later Carol joyfully reported her father was home. Her classmates clapped. They had experienced first-hand how concerned neighbors could help those less fortunate than themselves. From then on the Rizenburg children attended regularly.

By the middle of April the seventh and eighth graders had taken and passed their state tests. Now we could turn our attention to pleasant things.

"Last year we had more boys so we had fun playing baseball with other schools," Victor said. "Guess we'll have to do something different this year."

I looked from him to the girls who were listening. "Did you think about asking them to play ball?"

"Naw. They wear dresses."

I thought of all the years I'd worn overalls during the summer. "How about loaning your sister some overalls?"

"Pants won't help her." He grinned. "She couldn't hit a ball if it was as big as a watermelon."

When Martha heard that she nearly exploded. "I can hit as good as you can and I can run faster!"

Victor wrapped his arms around his head pretending to dodge a blow. "All right, you can wear a pair of my overalls, but I still say it won't help you hit a ball."

"Ha. You'll be sorry you said that." She turned to her friends. "Will you wear overalls tomorrow?"

Mary and Carol said they would, but Pauline hesitated. "I'd look taller than ever. I'd have to borrow a pair of Papa's."

"So will I," Mary said, "but I want to play."

The next morning the four girls came in overalls. The boys spent time showing them how to stand and how to hold a bat. A week later Jerry took us in his truck to challenge Nine Mile School. The final score was ten to zero in favor of the host team.

A week later we played Fairview School without much better success. After that game Jake suggested, "Let's do something else." The others agreed.

The following Friday we carried our lunches to the swamp. On the way we saw a meadow lark hopping along as though it had a broken wing. Victor ran ahead to catch it, but the bird kept a few feet ahead of him. When he returned to the group I suggested, "Now walk in the opposite direction from which the bird was going. I think you'll find her nest."

In a few minutes he motioned us to come. One by one we stooped down to look into a carefully concealed nest which was covered with an arched roof. There we saw two white speckled eggs.

"Are they all she'll lay?" Mary asked.

"Perhaps not. I've seen nests with as many as seven eggs. Let's go now. In a few weeks there'll be more birds singing 'Spring is here. Spring is here!' I think it's one of the prettiest songs I've ever heard."

Just as we reached the swamp we heard a splash. "Look!" Harry yelled. "I saw a beaver go underwater and here's the tree he was chewing on!"

A half hour later the children and I sat in a pretty green meadow eating our lunches. We watched the red-winged blackbirds flit from cattail to cattail chirping their cheery songs. The pupils planned the pictures they'd draw and paint on our return to the classroom. On the way back to school we picked flowers and enough cattails to make an attractive bouquet.

The art work was so well done I suggested we have a Mother's Day tea and invite the women in the community to view the exhibit. The older girls baked cookies and the boys pooled their money to purchase lemons and sugar for lemonade. My mother, the County Superintendent, and fifteen others arrived at one o'clock on the day we'd chosen.

Mrs. Schaffer spoke on behalf of the ladies. "Your display is excellent. I especially like the framed paintings done with watercolors on glass. We thank you for having us to this lovely party."

After the guests were gone and we were rearranging the room, George asked, "Miss Adams, what are we doing the last day of school?"

"Would you like to have a picnic at my parents' ranch?" I asked. "The water in Lake Alice is too cold for swimming, but you can go wading. If you go there, I'll have a surprise or two for you."

The children clapped. "Goody-goody!"

Martha threw her arms around me. "I'm so glad you're our teacher. We get to do lots of interesting things."

I smiled and hugged her back.

The last week dragged. It seemed as though Friday would never come. When it did, Jerry and Belle arrived at nine-thirty and away we went in their truck for the twelve-mile trip.

On the way Pauline asked, "What color is your house?"

"Sorta brown. It's never been painted."

She frowned. "Really? Why not?"

"That's one of my surprises. Wait and see."

When we drove into the yard the children shouted, "It's a house made of dirt!"

"Yes, it's a sod house."

Mother and Dad were waiting to greet us. The children scrambled from the truck and ran to put their hands on the sides of the house.

"Where did you get the sod?" Harry asked.

Dad pointed toward the east. "Up near that hill. It's called blackroot because the roots of the grass are intertwined in the earth so thick it holds the soil together."

"Was it hard to make?"

"Not very. I used a plow to turn over the sod, then cut it in eighteen-inch lengths. I laid them one on top of the other using them like bricks to form the walls."

Dad seemed pleased he was getting so much attention and was surprised the children were so interested. "Are there any more questions?"

"How long did it take to build it?" Jake asked.

"Nearly two months. We moved in just before Christmas. We'd been living in two tents for sixteen months."

Pauline turned a surprised face to me. "Then you're a pioneer."

I laughed. "Yes, I guess I am. Now let's give Mother a chance to show us the inside. Follow me."

As they walked from room to room Mother explained, "You notice how cool it is. Since the walls are three feet thick our home is cool in summer and warm in winter."

"I like the wallpaper," Mary said.

"Thank you. Once a lady from Philadelphia visited us. She seemed amazed to find the inside looks like most other houses."

As the children left to follow me to the ice pit, Pauline said, "Thank you, Mrs. Adams. I like your house."

Every winter when the ice in Lake Alice was at least three feet thick Dad and Norman cut it into two foot blocks, brought it on a sled, and packed straw around it as they stacked one layer on another until the pit was full. We could make ice cream every day if we wanted to.

Jake watched with interest when I removed some straw to expose a piece of ice. "I didn't know you could have your own ice. We buy ours from a plant in town."

"Have you any more surprises?" Martha asked as the children sat on the lawn in the front yard.

"One more." I went into the house and came out wearing a pair of black wooden shoes I'd just received from Henry's parents in Holland.

"These are what Dutch people wear on Sunday. Their everyday ones aren't painted. When they go indoors they leave their shoes on the step. They wear soft leather-soled slippers or heavy socks in the house."

"What do kids do at school?" George asked.

"The same thing. Just imagine what a quiet room they must have."

Harry laughed. "Does the teacher do that, too?"

"Henry told me most of them do."

After I removed the shoes the boys took turns wearing them. They were so large and clumsy most of the boys fell when they tried to walk.

Victor looked at the bottom when he took them off.

"No wonder they don't fit. This one is size seventy-nine." He picked up the other. "And this one is eighty-one."

We all laughed.

I looked at my watch. "It's time to get your lunches. We'll walk to the lake where those who wish may wade before we eat."

At one o'clock we climbed into the truck to start our return trip. Several children said they wished they lived near the lake. Pauline remarked, "I don't think our parents will believe all the things Jake and I are going to tell them." The others agreed.

When we reached the school the children and I thanked the Hays for taking us.

"Don't thank us," Jerry said. "We thank you. It was a fun time for everyone. I bet you kids will never forget this day."

Belle gave me a hug. "Treva, you've been a great teacher. Now I know you're going to have a new adventure. Jerry and I wish you a happy married life."

I swallowed. It suddenly struck me that time was rushing on. I looked at my watch. "It won't be long now. By eight o'clock tonight I'll be Mrs. Henry Ottjes."

"Tonight!" Mary exclaimed. "You're getting married tonight?" Their expressions showed how surprised they were.

"Yes, tonight. And this summer you're all invited to come to visit me."

I glanced again at the clock. Time really was fleeting. As I handed the children their report cards they hugged, kissed me and shook my hand. Finally I was alone.

Henry was to come at four o'clock. As I surveyed the room for the last time, I heard a familiar honk.

"You're right on the dot," I said as I came out the door.

"Yes, hurry and jump in. No one is looking, so I don't have to open the door for you."

He gave me a quick kiss and we were on our way to the courthouse to get our marriage license. About two blocks from our destination Henry stopped the car, got out and walked around to my side. He opened the door and said, "Move over. You will drive me there."

I looked at him in amazement, but didn't move. He used both hands to push me into the driver's seat.

"Why all this silliness?" I gave him a stern look.

With a twinkle in his eyes he said, "You will drive me to the slaughter and tonight I will be slaughtered."

"Oh, no you won't." I started the motor, saw no one was coming in either direction on the two lane road, turned the car around and headed back to Scottsbluff.

"Treva, Treva! What are you doing?"

"I'm going back to my apartment, get my car and go home."

By this time we were approaching the bridge over the North Platte River.

"You can't do this. Stop the car. I didn't mean it. Treva, stop the car. It's nearly five o'clock. The courthouse will soon close. We must get there."

I drove to the side of the road and stopped.

"Henry, marriage is no laughing matter. If you really want to marry me, you drive to the courthouse."

He jumped from the car and ran to the other side. There was no time to discuss the subject if we were to get our license before closing time.

I didn't remember seeing Henry so perplexed. This time he didn't have a wise or silly saying. As we headed toward our destination all he said over and over was, "I'm sorry."

We were quiet as we entered the courthouse, signed for our license, and returned to the car. He opened the door, I stepped in, and he went around to the driver's side. He sat beside me and took me in his arms. At first both of us were tense and then we relaxed as we clung to each other.

"You are so right and I was wrong to tease you. I love you so much." He gently kissed away the tears that streamed down my cheeks.

"I know, but Henry, there are times when your silliness has gone too far and this was sure one of them."

A few minutes later we straightened in our seats. Then slowly he reached into an inside jacket pocket and took out a small box. "Hold out your left hand."

He gently removed my engagement ring with the small diamond. "I think this is better for you."

My eyes widened in surprise as he placed on my finger a ring with a stone three times the size of the other.

"It's so big and beautiful!" Now it was my turn to hug and kiss him. "You do bewilder me sometimes, I confess, but this ring shows you want me for your wife and I promise to be a good one."

"I know you will." He opened a second box. "This is the wedding ring with seven diamonds that I'll put on your finger tonight."

With that he started the motor and we were on our way.